# The Network Balancing Act: Ensuring Performance and Sustainability in the Age of Big Data

Molina

# CONTENTS

# CHAPTER 1

# INTRODUCTION

The rapid development of Information and Communication Technologies (ICT) have fundamentally changed human's daily life and driven the modern society into the era of big data. The triumph of mobile devices, owned in 2017 by more than 5 billion people [1], allows uploading videos and photos to social media for *"the needs to belong and self-presentation"* [163]. The 26.6 billion connected devices and sensors [105] belonging to Internet of Things (IoT) continuously monitor our environment and provide data to support applications like smart home [238] and healthcare [176]. These services and applications generate enormous amount of data to collect, transmit and process. The Cisco Visual Networking Index forecasts that the volumn of traffic data generated by mobile devices, including smartphones and IoT devices, is going to reach 40 Exabytes ($10^9$ Gigabytes) by the year 2021 [42], and the annual global IP traffic will grow to 4.8 Zettabytes ($10^{12}$ Gigabytes) by the year 2022 [41]. The transmission of such high data volumes places heavy burdens on the networking infrastructure in almost every phase of the data handling [26], which urges networks in the future to be agile, high-performance and secure.

Networks provide the facility resources to forward and process data for network users, while maintaining the functioning of devices causes the operational costs for network owners. The network facility resources commonly refer to the communication bandwidth to forward data packets [30] and computation capacity to perform operations on data packets [171]. The purpose of network facility resource management is to maximize the resource utilization so as to increase the system's efficiency during processing of packets. The network performance, that is captured by the Quality of Service (QoS) parameters, degrades if network facility resource such as bandwidth is not efficiently allocated. At the same time, the functioning network facilities lead to large amount of operational costs. Besides the personnel expenditure to maintain the network infrastructure, the energy cost can contribute to over 15% of the overall Operating Expenditure (Opex) of the backbone networks [181]. The four major US telecom companies – AT&T, Verizon, Sprint and T-Mobile – consumes over 3 million MWh of electric power [81], which leads to the high Opex for the network owners. In this book, we refer the problem of efficiently utilizing the network facility resources and reducing the operational cost as the resource efficiency problem in a network.

The concept of resource efficiency exists in different functional planes of a network. A network usually has three functional planes [182]: (i) the data plane that operates on data packets for forwarding and filtering; (ii) the control plane that decides the states, such as forwarding decisions, in the data plane; (iii) the monitoring plane that continuously monitor and analyze network traffic and devices. In order to build an efficient and sustainable network, performing optimization on the utilization of corresponding resources in each of these three planes is necessary.

Software Defined Networking (SDN) allows to dynamically change the configurations of network devices, e.g., switches or routers, based on centrally collected operational information in a network. It provides the great flexility to perform Traffic Engineering (TE) and control the behaviours of data flows in the network. Several approaches tackle the resource efficiency problem in a network by intelligently scheduling, for example, the routing paths for data flows, as well as determining the configurations and states of the involved hardware and software components [32, 98, 204, 208, 246, 251].

This book contributes novel models and algorithms to improve the ability of SDN networks to adapt to changing network conditions and performance requirements. The ultimate goal of such adaptation is to achieve the resource efficiency in the above mentioned functional planes of a network. The developed techniques are meant to run in a centralized SDN controller. Since this controller becomes a single point of failure due to the abusive usage of the control plane resource, we also contribute an approach to protect the control plane resource against certain security threats.

## 1.1 MOTIVATION AND CHALLENGES

Improving the resource efficiency has been a widely discussed topic in the networking community. As an important aspect of network management, approaches based on TE provide the possibility to intelligently manage the operation status of network devices and utilize available network facility resources, without compromising the service quality of networks. The basic principle of conserving network resources and reducing its cost via TE is twofold: (i) utilize available network resources in an efficient way; (ii) serve desired communication demands with minimum cost. The existing literature presents a plethora of models and algorithms to improve network resource utilization and reduce cost like energy [98, 148, 246] or bandwidth [32, 204, 208] in SDN networks. These approaches prove that TE-based methods have the potential to achieve the resource efficiency in the data, control and monitoring planes in SDN. These TE-based methods take the advantage of the centralized architecture of SDN and its capability to perform network and traffic planning according to the communication demands of applications that transmit data.

As the newly developed technologies and emerging applications continuously integrate with the architecture of SDN, the diversity of hardware used in the network and applications generating data flows, makes it a complex task to achieve secure and efficient utilization of resource in the functional planes of SDN. Newly arising scenarios require previously developed the models and algorithms to be adapted to work under different assumptions. The work presented in this book inherits the idea of designing models and algorithms based on traffic engineering, to enhance the adaptivity of resource-efficient SDN when facing challenges described below.

**Challenge 1:** *Dynamic network conditions and optimization requirements*
The optimality of a configuration for a communication network cannot be always guaranteed at runtime. This is due to the increasing dynamics within the network. The common sources of such dynamics include but are not limited to: (i) changing conditions in the network (e.g., data transmission workloads); (ii) diverse co-existing requirements in the application scenarios (e.g., energy efficiency as well as congestion avoidance). Data communication demands and traffic patterns within networks are volatile in both the space and time domains [20], making it necessary for a network controller to be aware of current network conditions. Additionally, focusing solely on improving the resource efficiency could bring negative impacts on the quality of services, due to the scarce resources that are available for data flows. Normally, diverse requirements, such as end-to-end delays and transmission reliability, co-exist with the target of network resource efficiency. As a result, a network controller must be able to obtain or predict network conditions and to dynamically adjust its configurations to maintain the resource efficiency while meeting the desired service qualities of network services.

**Challenge 2:** *Joint optimization across network layers*
The concept of designing programmable network devices does not impact only the way of packet processing as commonly known in the standard of SDN protocols [150]. It also influences the functioning of all protocols, from the network physical layer to the application layer. The term SDN can generally refer to an integrated solution that handles different layers of a network and consists of several software defined technologies such as Software Defined Radio (SDR) [218], Software Defined Antenna (SDA) [122] and Software Defined Network Functionality Virtualization (SD-NFV) [135]. These key enabling technologies for software-defined, highly configurable networks can integrate with each other easily because they all rely on a centralized software control mechanism [233]. Performing optimization in such software-defined environment with heterogeneous technologies requires considering the dependencies of the different network layers. For instance, in distributed big data processing frameworks, planning the locations of each individual task and bandwidth allocated along routing paths for data transferring among those tasks has the potential to speed up data movement [177]. In addition, for the purpose of resource and cost reduction, a network management system cannot only rely on traffic engineering to make the routing decisions, because the network performance degrades severely without proper coordinations of the actions taken in multiple layers [197]. For example, the routing paths planned for traffic flows should not include the devices in sleep mode, otherwise packets may expe-

rience large end-to-end delays [115]. As a result, the developed approaches should follow the methodology of *joint optimization* across network layers, so that the configurations of a layer do not conflict with that of another layer.

**Challenge 3:** *Large configuration and solution space*
In this book, the goal of the TE-based joint optimization approaches is to find a combination of network configurations, possibly including hardware operation states, routing paths of data flows and placement of top-layer applications, so as to reduce the resource consumption in SDN. However, the search space of possible solutions can be very large because of: (i) the growing size of target SDN networks (horizontal), (ii) the increasing number of reconfiguration opportunities in the heterogeneous SDN environment (vertical). A data center could consist of up to $60,000$ hosts that are connected by a large-scale network [175]. The network controller must thus deal with high volumes of transmission demands of data flows generated by these many hosts. Additionally, as mentioned in the description of Challenge 2, the heterogeneous SDN environment is built upon various software defined technologies, and performing joint optimization requires to coordinate configurations across network layers. To reduce the computation delay, the algorithms need to, at runtime, quickly find the network configuration that leads to the resource efficiency from a large solution space.

**Challenge 4:** *Vulnerable centralized controller*
An essential property of SDN is logical centralization of network management functionalities. Typically, network configuration algorithms and models reside in one of the many controller applications sharing the computation and network resource of the control channel. Although the scalability and resilience of the SDN control plane are improved by using multiple synchronized controller instances [113], the logically centralized controller still faces threats from illegitimate or abusive usage of the SDN paradigm [5]. The attacks, which targets on exhausting limited yet valuable control plane resources, e.g., computation and bandwidth, disrupt the obtaining of network state data and calculation of management strategies.

To address these challenges in achieving the resource efficiency in the functional planes of SDN, a network and flow management framework, that is capable of monitoring network states and controlling the network behaviours, is envisioned in this book. In particular, this framework monitors the operation status of a network and analyzes traffic flow packets to extract information to support traffic engineering and other configurations. To perform resource-efficient scheduling, it accepts real-time flow requests or predicted flow patterns. This envisioned framework allows different optimization tasks for the resource utilization of the functional planes of SDN. We focus on the design of the resource-efficient scheduling models and algorithms residing in this framework. Corresponding to the challenges presented above, we identify four common requirements on such a network flow management framework and its resource-efficient scheduling models and algorithms:

- *Self-adaptive.* The dynamic network conditions, such as data flow workloads, require the scheduling algorithms to be able to compute resource-efficient configurations adaptively. The computation relies on either explicitly received communication demands in future time slots or implicitly inferred traffic patterns. When communication demands or traffic patterns evolve in real-time, the framework should be able to respond to their changes by automatically adjusting the parameters of its model or algorithm.

- *Responsive.* It takes time for the framework to obtain network states, calculate network management strategies according to collected information, and finally send control messages to configure networks. Although our framework does not intend to speed up the propagation of monitoring and control messages, it indeed requires efficient algorithms to improve the responsiveness of the controller to reduce the delays experienced by flow packets.

- *Flexible.* The diverse requirements in application scenarios demand the framework to be flexible so as to solve various resource optimization tasks. Meanwhile, the traffic engineering and management algorithms rely on diverse mathematical models. Thus, the framework should allow easy integration of different models and algorithms to compare their performance.

- *Secure.* Potential malicious users can take advantage of the centralized architecture of SDN and abuse the computation and bandwidth resources of the control channel. In order to improve the resilience and security of the controller that performs resource-efficient scheduling in SDN, the framework should contain a security mechanism against malicious users at runtime.

## 1.2 RESEARCH GOALS AND CONTRIBUTIONS

The main goal of this book is to contribute novel algorithms, that run in a protected controller, to perform cross-layer optimization on the resource consumption in several functional planes, including data, control and monitoring planes, of SDN. Figure 1.1 provides an overview and depicts the main components of the book contributions[1]. In this book, we start with designing a resource-efficient packet flow monitoring system for the

---

[1] The research presented in this book is funded by the Deutsche Forschungsgemeinschaft (DFG) projects "Multi-Mechanisms Adaptation for the Future Internet (MAKI) [144]" and "Highly Adaptive Energy-Efficient Computing (HAEC)" [86].

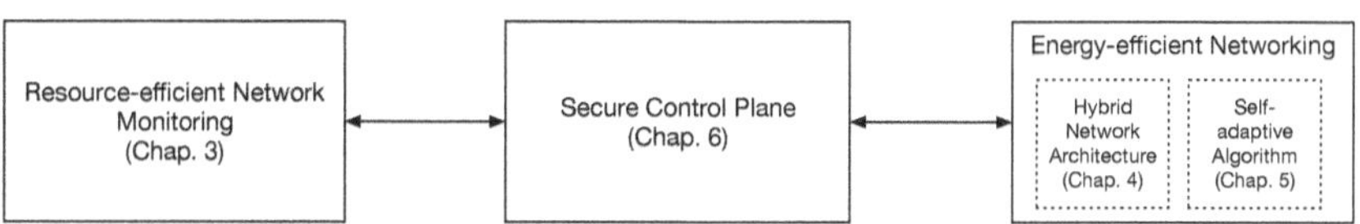


*Figure 1.1:* Overview and components of book contributions

purposes of collecting flow statistics and deep packet inspection. The controller not only receives monitoring results, but also performs traffic engineering and configuration of this monitoring system so as to reduce the overall bandwidth consumption. The collected flow statistics, together with explicitly communicated QoS demands of applications, serve as input data to further optimize the energy consumption of SDN networks. In particular, to improve the adaptivity of the centralized scheduling controller, we design algorithms for heterogeneous SDN integrated with different communication technologies and investigate self-adaptive algorithms based on Deep Reinforcement Learning (DRL). Additionally, we use the in-network approach to construct a secure control plane to protect the centralized controller, without incurring waste of control channel resources. We describe these contributions in more details below.

### 1.2.1 *Resource-efficient Network Monitoring*

The first contribution of this book is a network flow monitoring solution that performs packet inspection on the predefined set of data flows. This solution is named REMO, which stands for **Resource Efficient distributed MO**nitoring. In the current deployment of SDN networks, the forwarding devices, such as switches or virtual network functions, can be configured to duplicate and forward the packets of selected data flows to a packet monitor. The original data flows and duplicated data flows are separately transmitted in the data plane and monitoring plane to increase the transmission reliability of the monitoring system. This solution, however, incurs high transmission costs in the network. In REMO, the SDN controller performs a joint optimization of the placement of network monitors, routing paths of original data flows and selection of locations to duplicate data flows. Comparing with similar approaches, REMO does not only consider the resource reduction in the monitoring plane, but takes the negative impacts (increased resource consumption) in the data plane into consideration. This contribution has appeared in the following publication:

- T. Li, H. Salah, M. He, T. Strufe and S. Santini: "REMO: Resource Efficient Distributed Network Monitoring", in Proceeding of the IEEE Network Operations and Management Symposium (NOMS), April, 2018.

### 1.2.2 *Reduce resource consumption for heterogeneous SDN*

The second contribution of this book is a centralized flow routing path planning and network topology management solution to reduce the power consumption of SDN networks. This solution is named ECAS, which stands for **E**nergy-aware **C**oflow and **A**ntenna **S**cheduling. This solution is designed for software-defined Data Center Networking (DCN) equipped with heterogeneous communication mediums, namely wired links and high-frequency wireless links. ECAS achieves energy efficiency by: (i) aggregating traffic flows so as to limit the number of activated nodes and links; (ii) taking the advantage of "shortcuts" formed by directional wireless links so as to involve even fewer active nodes and links. We show the NP-Hardness of the problem and develop a heuristic algorithm to compute a network configuration within milliseconds. This contribution was presented in the following publications:

- T. Li and S. Santini: "Energy-aware Coflow and Antenna Scheduling for Hybrid Server-centric Data Center Networks", in Proceeding of the IEEE International Conference on Communication (ICC), May 2017. (Transmission, Access and Optical Systems (TAOS) Best Paper Award and Green Communications & Computing (TCGCC) Best Paper Award)

- T. Li and S. Santini: "Energy-aware Coflow and Antenna Scheduling for Hybrid Server-centric Data Center Networks", in IEEE Transaction on Green Communication and Networks, 3.2 (2019), pp. 356–365.

### 1.2.3 *Resource optimization using self-adaptive algorithms*

Existing solutions that optimize the resource efficiency, such as the power consumption, mainly rely on the formulation of an optimization problem and the design of heuristic algorithms. The formulated model and algorithm usually remain static and requires reformulation for new network topologies or evolving traffic workloads. In addition, due to the hard constraints in the problem formulation, not every possible input value can lead to a valid solution. To improve the adaptivity of the controller that optimizes the power efficiency of SDN, we investigated the possibility to use the approach based on deep reinforcement learning. The actions produced by the algorithm are network configurations that lead to reduction of power consumption in a SDN-based data center network. We show that, despite the very cumbersome training processes, DRL based scheduling approaches are able to optimize the power consumption of a regular data center network based on SDN to some extent. Parts of this contribution have been presented in:

- T. Li, T. Strufe, and S. Santini. "MADeep-TE: A multi-agent reinforcement learning approach for network traffic engineering," Prepared to submit to the IEEE International Conference on Communication Technology (ICCT), 2020.

### 1.2.4  *In-network protection scheme for SDN control plane*

The last contribution of this book is an in-network protection scheme for the SDN control plane. A well-known approach to disrupt the SDN control plane is to initiate Denial of Service (DoS) attacks by deliberately generating large amount of control messages. Most existing countermeasure approaches require a module residing on the controller side. In these approaches, illegitimate control messages still need to be be firstly transmitted from switches to the controller, which incurs consumption of valuable control plane bandwidth. We propose INFAS, an in-network protection scheme, that is executed directly next to switches, to filter out packets that possibly belong to malicious network users. INFAS does not seek to completely block all packets of a flow that generates many control messages. Instead, in order to also handle workload peaks, it allows to configure different dropping rates for passing packets, depending on the realtime monitoring results. Parts of this contribution have been already published in:

- T. Li, H. Salah, D. Xin, T. Strufe, F. H. P. Fitzek, and S. Santini, "INFAS: In-network flow management scheme for SDN control plane protection," in Proceedings of the IEEE/IFIP Integrated Network Management Symposium (IM), April 2019.

## 1.3  THESIS ORGANIZATION

The remainder of this book is structured as follows: Chapter 2 introduces the concept of software-defined networking and SDN-assisted traffic engineering, and it also introduces three major challenges in conserving or protecting resources in different functional planes of SDN. We also summarize the related work that focuses on these three major challenges of protecting and efficiently utilizing resource in SDN. Chapter 3 presents REMO, a resource efficient monitoring framework that intends to reduce the overall bandwidth consumption for both data and monitoring planes. Chapter 4 and Chapter 5 address the power resource reduction in the data plane but focus on different aspects: (i) Chapter 4 presents ECAS, a joint energy-efficient scheduling framework to plan both the physical topology and flow paths in a hybrid SDN network; (2) Chapter 5 focuses on using a type of self-adaptive algorithms, deep reinforcement learning, to optimize the power consumption for a SDN data center networks of the fat-tree topology. In Chapter 6, we develop a protection mechanism to mitigate abusive usage of the control plane resource in SDN. Finally, we summarize the achieved results, discuss limitations and possible future directions in Chapter 7.

CHAPTER 2

---

# BACKGROUND AND RELATED WORK

---

In this chapter, we provide the readers with background and related work for the contributions of this book. We start by introducing the SDN technology and discuss how it can be extended to perform cross-layer optimization in a softwarized network in Section 2.1. Section 2.2 further provides an overview of traffic engineering and the basic architecture of a SDN-assisted traffic engineering framework. The contributions presented in this book tackle the resource conservation issues of three functional planes in a SDN network, namely the monitoring plane, data plane and control plane. As a result, Section 2.3 provides the overview of the corresponding solutions based on SDN-assisted traffic engineering.

## 2.1 SOFTWARE DEFINED NETWORKING

Communication networks are defined as a collection of *autonomous* computing devices that are interconnected so as to exchange information [210]. The autonomy of communication devices implies that they operate with distributed network control and transport protocols. The protocols running on devices make transmission decisions based on information that is locally collected or exchanged with neighboring devices. The widely used Internet routing protocol, Open Shortest Path First (OSPF), is an example of such a distributed network protocol [161]. In OSPF, each router maintains a database that contains link state information exchanged among adjacent devices. From the perspective of devices' functional planes, autonomous networking devices have tightly-coupled control and data planes that are *vertically* integrated [6]. The design of distributed network protocols improves the availability and robustness of networks [58].

However, as growing communication scenarios (e.g., large-sized data centers) inspire the development of new network protocols, the paradigm of designing protocols relying on vertically integrated functionality planes exhibits the major shortcoming: complexity. Benson *et al.* [19] point out that the management complexity of a network consisting of autonomous devices comes from: (i) the efforts to configure large volumes of devices; (2) the *"inherent complexity"* of implementing control policies and customizing them for network devices with distinct roles. Especially when facing continually changing network states, it is cumbersome for network operators to manually adjust configurations of devices [119].

In addition to the complexity brought by using fully distributed networking devices, the currently adopted network architecture also suffers from the problem of rigidity. The tightly coupled data and control planes make it difficult to change the network architecture. And a rigid network architecture does not allow extensibility of a new network functionality such as a flexible routing system [77].

Additionally, static and rigid bundling of the hardware and software of networking devices only allows a network to be controlled by *"the proprietary protocols of a specific vendor"* [200]. Modern communication networks face a dynamic environment in which traffic workloads, application demands and architecture evolve. A network should have *adaptivity* and *flexibility* to adjust its configurations according to these dynamics so as to maintain its functional and non-functional performance. In the DFG project "Multi-Mechanisms Adaptation for the Future Internet (MAKI)", the network adaptivity is achieved by dynamically selecting network protocols during runtime [144].

The ongoing network softwarization, which relies on software to control networking behaviors and to implement networking functions, contributes to the adaptivity and flexibility of communication networks [97].

### 2.1.1 *Software defined networking architecture*

SDN is a novel control paradigm that brings more agility and flexibility into network management. In the early stage of SDN research, SDN is usually considered as a synonym of the OpenFlow protocol for wired networks [150], that defines interfaces to instruct the behaviors of switches or routers.

Adaptively steering flows is part of the early research efforts that explore the benefits brought by SDN. Hedera [67] and Mahout [50] are two traffic load-balancing approaches. Both Hedera and Mahout have a monitoring component detecting and estimating the volumes of so-called *elephant flows*, i.e., flows that contain large volumes of data packets. The difference is that, Hedera obtains flow statistics from edge switches while Mahout collects such information by locally monitoring socket buffers of end hosts. The SDN controllers of both frameworks react to the existence of elephant flows and intelligently assign non-conflicting paths for them.

RFC 7426 [87] gives a more general definition of SDN: *"a new approach for network programmability, that is, the capacity to initialize, control, change, and manage network behavior dynamically via open interfaces"*. Feamster et al. [69] trace the origin of SDN back to the concept of *active networking* proposed in the early- to mid-1990s. This approach advocates a set of programming interfaces that expose the resources (e.g., processing and storage) of network nodes and support the installation of customized packet processing functionality onto them. Compared with the early efforts of enhancing network programmability, such as active networking, SDN distinguishes itself by decoupling control and data planes. More

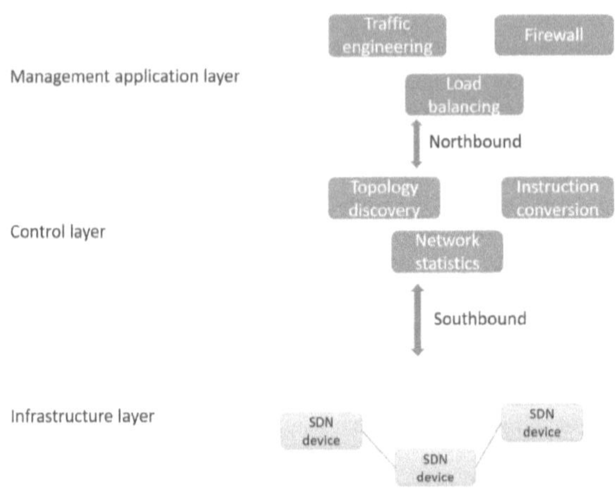


*Figure 2.1:* Layers of a typical software defined network, inspired by [27].

specifically, in SDN, network control logics run in an external entity that interacts with underlying data plane devices to program behavior of a network [69, 87, 126]. As a result, the term, SDN, can generally refer to a network architecture with this property. Figure 2.1 shows the layers of a typical software-defined network, and the functionality of each layer is described as following:

- *Infrastructure layer.* This layer consists of devices that are interconnected with either wireless or wired channels and performs elementary operations on received data frames or packets [126]. The devices in the infrastructure layer do not run complex distributed network protocols. Instead, their control policies are implemented in an external entity in a logically centralized manner.

- *Control layer.* A SDN controller resides in this layer and programs devices in the infrastructure layer. Due to the logically centralized architecture, a SDN controller provides services (e.g., topology discovery and simple traffic workload counting) to collect and maintain global information of network states. These network-wide information can be obtained by management applications such as network monitoring. The control layer is also responsible of converting the abstract policies generated by management applications to the elementary operation set understood by SDN devices in the lower layer.

| Match fields | Priority | Counters | Instructions | Timeouts | Cookies | Flags |
| --- | --- | --- | --- | --- | --- | --- |

*Figure 2.2:* Structure of a flow rule defined in the OpenFlow protocol.

- *Management application layer.* This layer comprises of a set of network management applications such as a load balancer and a gateway. The models and algorithms that perform traffic engineering on data flows are also implemented as the part of this layer.

We use the packet forwarding process defined in the OpenFlow protocol to illustate the interactions among these functional layers of SDN. Each switch in the infrastructure layer has a flow table to store its configuration in the form of flow rules. Figure 2.2 shows the presentations of a flow rule defined in the OpenFlow protocol. Each of these rules consists of a flow matching field and actions to match and process a received packet. When a flow packet arrives at a switch, the switch looks for a matching flow rule in its flow table. If found, the switch simply performs the corresponding actions (e.g., forward, modify, or drop). Otherwise, the switch sends a control packet to the controller in the control layer to consult for the actions to perform on the incoming flow packets. The routing module, for instance, in the management application layer obtains relevant information, such as the source/destination of flow packets, from the controller and compute a flow path for these packets. In turn, the controller replies with another control packet containing a flow rule. The switch stores the received rule in its flow table and handles the flow packet accordingly. Particularly in OpenFlow, the switch consults the controller through a packet_in message which summarizes the header of the unmatched flow packet. The controller responds either with an ofp_flow_mod message to add or modify flow rules, or with a packet_out message to instruct the switch to forward the packet to a specific port.

SDN has become a crucial technology to revolutionize network management. It provides network owners with great flexibility by defining standard interfaces for configuring operational status of networking devices and allowing implementation of network management policies in a logically centralized controller. SDN has shown its capability to improve network performance, including link congestion reduction and power conservation, in a controllable environment such as data centers [92, 109]. In recent years, SDN has also gradually gained popularity in Wide Area Network (WAN) [83, 184] and Mobile Core Network (MCN) [147, 165].

The main purpose of this book is to develop mechanisms and algorithms to effectively reduce resource consumption in multiple layers of a computer network. Because of the flexibility of programming network behaviors and the central view over network states, we select SDN as the fundamental technology to develop the novel algorithms for this purpose.

### 2.1.2 *Cross-layer network control*

Network softwarization is often referred as the integration of Software Defined Networking (SDN) and Network Functionality Virtualization (NFV) [52, 117]. Among the network softwarization technologies, SDN mainly serves the purpose of enhancing the network flexibility in flow configuration in the network layer [97]. NFV refers to the concept of using application-based networking functions instead of dedicated hardware [96]. In most of the time, flow configuration in SDN refers to *"creation, removal or adaptation of the course of flows"* [97]. The functionality of flow configuration actually belongs to a broader concept, Traffic Engineering. We will introduce the concept of TE in Section 2.2.

In recent research efforts, the concept of SDN evolves from two aspects: (i) extending the current SDN protocol to convey additional control information so as to change the operation status of software or hardware components; (ii) integrating SDN with other centralized management frameworks of software and hardware components, since SDN is one of the fundamental technologies supporting network softwarization. In this case, as we briefly discussed in Section 1.1, flow configuration, together with parameter configuration and operation status of software and hardware, should be jointly considered to further optimize network performance. The solutions developed in this book to reduce the consumption of network resources, not only steer traffic in an adaptive manner but also determine component states, such as the locations of network monitors or the physical topology. In this section, we provide an overview and examples on using SDN to perform cross-layer optimization.

#### 2.1.2.1 *Network control using SDN and software component management*

One of the features of SDN is allowing a network controller to interact with running software entities that use the network to transmit data. Information is shared via their channels in both directions. This feature makes it possible to design and build *application-aware* networks [34, 99], *network-aware* applications [51, 177] and *joint optimization* approaches [7, 110, 156, 249]. In the era of cloud and big data, applications refer to big data processing applications (e.g., Hadoop [9], Spark [10]), multi-tenant cloud resource management (e.g., OpenStack [170]), or virtualized network functions [135]. These applications share the following similarities: (i) they consist of distributed software components requiring exchange of data; (ii) they have a centralized management point (e.g., the master node of Hadoop); (iii) they have demands for network resources and QoS requirements to transmit data; and (iv) their resource demands and requirements can be explicitly declared by application users. Applications with these properties have a single management point that can interface with a SDN controller to exchange status information and control messages [48, 222].

The concept of application-aware networks represents the integrated approaches in which a network controller accepts information of resource demands from applications and carefully configures networks to achieve network optimization goals. In the scheme named *Application-aware Resource Allocation* [99], the bandwidth requirements (together with other resource requirements such as CPU) of Virtual Machines (VMs) are firstly predicted using a neural network. A SDN controller uses the predicted bandwidth requirements to provision network resources. The concept of network-aware applications stands for the integrated approach in which an application manager obtains information of network states from a SDN controller and schedules execution of its distributed software components. BASS [177] can obtain real-time link bandwidth information from the SDN controller, and assign Hadoop tasks requiring data movement to the nodes having rich bandwidth. In addition, the joint optimization approaches coordinate configurations in both network and application layers so as to maximize the network efficiency and application performance. Alkaff et al. [7] consider cross-layer scheduling for big data processing frameworks in cloud computing to improve system throughput and reliability.

#### 2.1.2.2 *Network control using SDN and hardware component management*

If we simply refer SDN as the technology to manipulate packet flows in the network layer, then SDN devices are mostly switches or routers that forward packets [118]. The default transmission media, at least in most of the SDN-related literature, is based on the Ethernet technology. While a network may consist of various communication technologies, SDN should integrate and "*embrace all possible transmission media, including wired, wireless and optical environment*" [232]. For example, ÆtherFlow is an SDN framework for IEEE 802.11 (Wi-Fi) networks and a controller can configure a set of properties of an Access Point (AP) [236]. As we briefly mentioned in Section 1.1, Software Defined Radio (SDR) allows using software to control wireless transmission strategies in the physical layer. CrossFlow [197] is a framework that combines SDR and SDN to enable physical layer adaptation, QoS provisioning, adaptive routing and joint optimization across physical and networking layers. Here, we provide two examples related to our contributions: (1) topology adaptation and (2) power adaptation in a network.

The first example of SDN-based network and hardware management is topology adaptation. The above described network control using SDN and hardware component management enables hybrid network architectures in different scenarios, e.g., cloud data centers where network flexibility is needed. Traditionally, data center networks use an architecture based on the fat-tree topology, as shown in Figure 2.3. The connections among Top-of-Rack (ToR), aggregation and core switches are usually wired Ethernet connections. The tree-based DCN has the oversubscription problem, in which the aggregated bandwidth demands of servers may exceed the provided capacity of links in the network. To cope with this problem, several authors considered introducing wireless links into the design

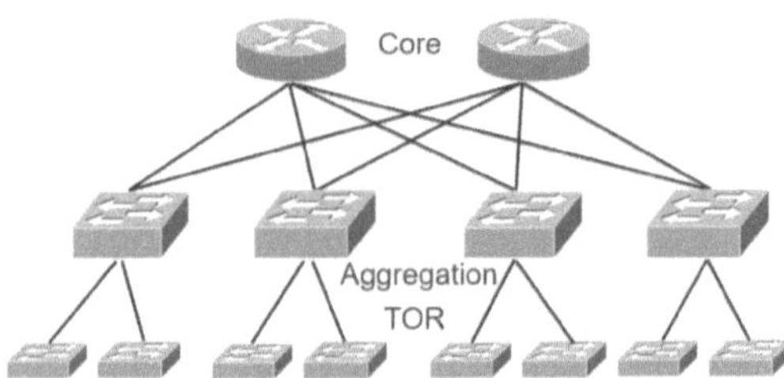


*Figure 2.3:* SDN network that has the typical fat-tree topology that only consists of Ethernet connections.

of DCN [88, 90]. Figure 2.4a depicts one of possible arrangement of coexisting wired and wireless links [88, 91, 228, 254]. In this DCN architecture, each ToR is equipped with a directional wireless transceiver that allows establishment of direct communication links among them by bypassing aggregation and core switches. The DFG project "Highly Adaptive Energy-Efficient Computing (HAEC)" envisions a micro data center architecture that involves diverse transmission media [70, 86], as shown in Figure 2.4b. In this architecture, a micro data center consists of multiple stacked layers. Each layer contains several computing nodes that are interconnected by wired/optical links. To enable flexible communication among stacked layers, each computing node also has a directional wireless transceiver that allows them to establish direct communication links.

For such DCN containing directional wireless links, the basic management tasks include: (i) monitoring and collecting traffic demands in networks; (ii) selecting a runtime topology by steering wireless transmitters and receivers to establish communication links; (iii) configuring forwarding paths for data flows [88, 89, 91, 228, 254]. More complex management tasks include channel allocation in the wireless spectrum [54]. In several proposed frameworks that focus on global management, a SDN architecture is assumed to support cross-layer data plane reconfiguration and enable efficient packet transmission in DCN.

The second example of using extension of SDN to configure networks shardware components is to adapt power consumption of devices, e.g., switches and routers, to conserve energy. It is due to the fact that modern networking devices allow using transmitted command packets to switch on/off the whole device or their components such as a specific line card even a port [55]. More granular control on networking devices' power states relies on the dynamic voltage and frequency scaling (DVFS) technique that adjusts the power and processing speed of devices' processor and peripheral circuit [55]. This technique enables systems that perform traffic flow path scheduling and link data rate configuration to avoid unnecessary power consumption spent on providing unused bandwidth as we discuss in Section 2.3.2. The cross-layer design, that jointly considers the hardware status and traffic

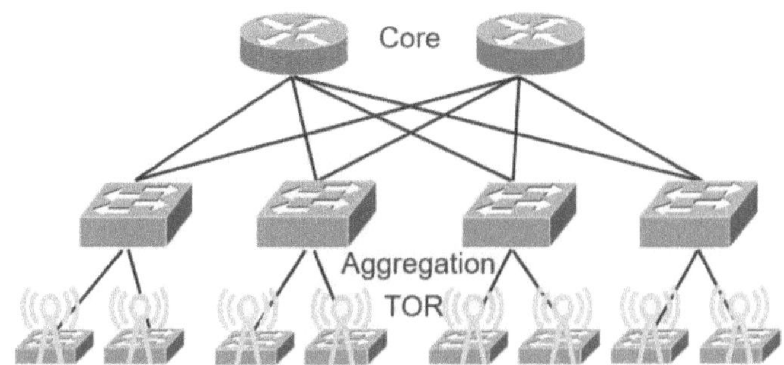



*(a)* Hybrid DCN architecture based on the traditional fat-tree topology.

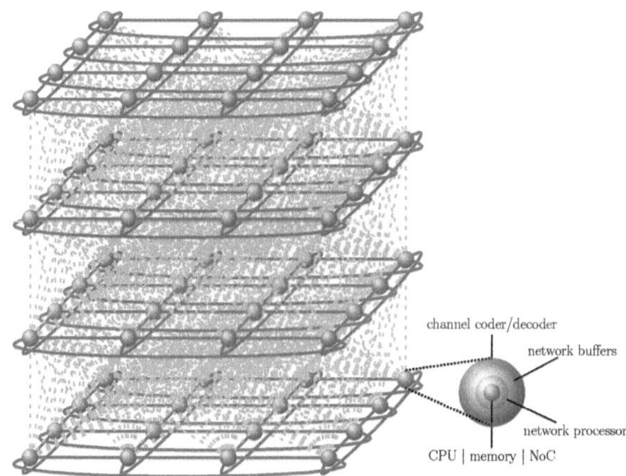



*(b)* Stacked computing cluster architecture envisioned in the DFG project "Highly Adaptive Energy-Efficient Computing (HAEC)" [86]. This figure is taken from its project proposal.

*Figure 2.4:* Two innovative DCN architectures that introduces directional wireless links.

engineering for data flows, is a basic idea to conserve power consumption in SDN for many frameworks, including the ones developed in Chapter 4 and Chapter 5.

## 2.2 TRAFFIC ENGINEERING BASED ON SDN

The term, Traffic Engineering, is typically used to indicate approaches that measure, analyze and regulate network traffic flows so as to improve the performance of data networks. Through the history of traffic engineering, many different supporting technologies, including SDN, have been developed to achieve this goal.

### 2.2.1 Basic concepts of traffic engineering

Traffic engineering achieves optimization of computer networks by addressing performance requirements of traffics and economically utilizing network resources. Lee and Mukherjee [132] describe the goal of TE as *"to put the data traffic where the network bandwidth is available in an efficient and effective way"*. According to RFC 3272 [11], the components of the traffic engineering process model include:

- *Measurement.* Measurement and monitoring provide operational states and environment changes of a network as the data basis to adapt network device and software configurations [214] to the traffic engineering control system. A network measurement and monitoring subsystem also provides feedback to evaluate the effectiveness of the carried out traffic engineering policies.

- *Modeling, Analysis and Simulation.* Performing modeling and analysis of network structures and behavior allows the abstract description of a network. These abstract models usually simplify the complexity of a network in reality. Despite of this drawback, researchers can still rely on these modeling and analysis results and use network simulators to test the performance of developed traffic engineering policies.

- *Optimization.* Optimizing network performance is a continuous process of identifying network issues, designing and implementation of corresponding solutions. Depending on the timescale of operations and granularity of actions, *real-time optimization* and *non-real-time planning* can be further distinguished.

The frameworks and approaches developed in this book follow the above design rules of traffic engineering. The presented resource-efficient monitoring framework and SDN control plane defense system perform measurement and monitoring on network traffic flows to provide data for characterizing workload statistics and identifying malicious packets. To optimize the bandwidth and power consumption, we formulate these problems using abstract models so that they can be solved by different mathematical tools and algorithms. In order to evaluate the performance of our developed optimization solutions, we developed simulation frameworks based on the models of the network structures and protocols in this book.

### 2.2.2 *Brief history of traffic engineering*

Traffic engineering has been an important research topic during the development of computer networks. Among all the essential aspects of traffic engineering, the functionality of routing, or flow path planning, plays an important role to enhance the network performance and improve their efficiency of resource utilization. The technologies that support the implementation of traffic engineering have continuously evolved during the past decades. The original purpose of traffic engineering in computer networks has been to alleviate network congestions since the late 1980s when Asynchronous Transfer Mode (ATM) networks became standard deployment in the telecommunications. In the 1990s, IP-based traffic engineering solutions gradually gained popularity over ATM-based solutions due to its independence of the physical transmission medium [120]. Traffic engineering methods, including routing protocols, are developed to ensure QoS requirements of traffics. In the late 1990s, Multiprotocol Label Switching (MPLS) became a frequently used technique in backbone networks to encapsulate IP packets to provide additional QoS guarantees. Hence, before the discussion of SDN-based traffic engineering (Section 2.2.3), we first provide brief introduction of traffic engineering performed in these predecessors of the SDN technology.

#### 2.2.2.1 *ATM-based TE*

ATM is a high-speed multiplexing and switching technique to support Broadband Integrated Services Digital Network (B-ISDN) [129, 179]. The main feature of ATM is that it is a connection-oriented networking architecture. In ATM-based networks, a Virtual Channel Connection (VCC) needs to be firstly established by two communication ends before actual transmission of fixed-sized data packets called *cells* [75]. ATM allows users to specify their desired QoS parameters, for example, Peak Cell Rate (PCR), Cell Loss Ratio (CLR), Cell Delay Variation (CDV), during the setup of a VCC [108]. ATM switches implement TE methods, such like admission control, bandwidth enforcement and traffic classification, to ensure the requested QoS demands can be satisfied [103].

#### 2.2.2.2 *IP-based TE*

Shifting from the connection-oriented network architecture of ATM to the best-effort network architecture of modern networks reduces the cost to construct and manage computer networks [125, 230]. This transition boosts the development of Internet following the Open Systems Interconnection (OSI) model that are now widespread. IP-based traffic engineering is a distributed approach and relies on Interior Gateway Protocol (IGP). The most widely used IGP protocols are Open Shortest Path First [160] and Intermediate System-Intermediate System (IS-IS) [199] that allow assignment of weight values to network links depending on the cost or workload of their connected links. Networking devices, like switches or routers, exchange link states with their neighbors so that the (constraint) shortest data flow paths can be computed and stored in the forwarding table. As a result, data paths can dynamically change and traffic engineering can achieve the goal of congestion avoidance and link failure recovery [80, 217].

### 2.2.2.3 *MPLS-based traffic engineering*

MPLS improves the packet forwarding efficiency over IP networks by matching routing entries based on packets' labels instead of the prefix of their IP addresses [22, 231]. MPLS supports flexible explicit routing that may divert from the shortest path to satisfy the resource requirements of a group of IP packets so called Forwarding Equivalence Class (FEC). The establishment of virtual tunnels, named Label-Switched Paths (LSPs), between the source and destination relies on the control plane signaling protocols to schedule routing paths and distribute labels.

The control plane protocols used in MPLS can be either *distributed* or *centralized*. Label Distribution Protocol (LDP) and Resource Reservation Protocol (RSVP) are common distributed MPLS control protocols, in which routers exchange signaling messages, e.g., label binding information [40]. Although LDP has the feature of easy configuration, RSVP is able to provide the traffic engineering functionality by signaling the devices along a routing path to reserve a certain amount of bandwidth resources for a FEC. The extended version of MPLS, the Generalized MPLS (GMPLS) architecture, defines a set of protocols and intends to provide a unified protocol for not only packet-based switching devices but also those in Wavelength Switched Optical Networks (WSONs) [145]. The idea of using a centralized controller, a dedicated Path Computation Element (PCE), to perform traffic engineering tasks (mainly routing), started to emerge [68, 106, 131]. In PCE/Generalized Multiprotocol Label Switching (GMPLS) for WSONs, the PCE monitor the network states and accepts path computation requests so as to dynamically compute lightpaths for packets [139].

### 2.2.3 *Traffic engineering assisted by SDN*

SDN enables flexible implementation of network management policies by providing programmable devices and unified interfaces to control them. Compared with the above mentioned network technologies, the essential characteristic of SDN – i.e., the separation of the control plane from the data plane and aggregation of management functions into a central entity – benefits traffic engineering from the following aspects:

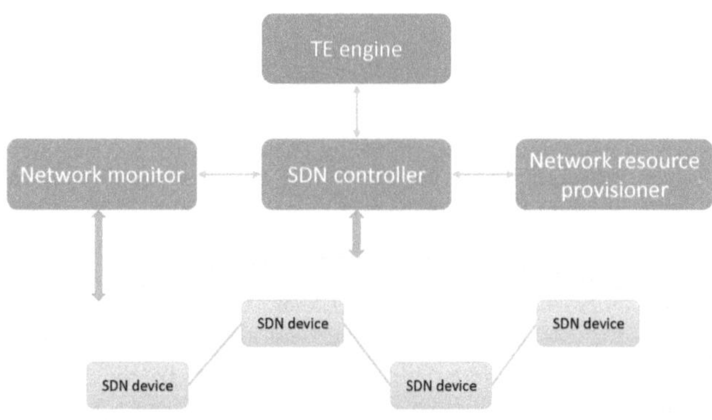

*Figure 2.5:* Components of a traffic engineering system assisted by SDN.

- The centralized architecture in SDN allows the acquisition and storage of global network states. For example, the network topology information can be obtained via the centralized version of Link Layer Discovery Protocol (LLDP) [13]. The SDN controller can use the OpenFlow protocol to query switches' flow table so as to learn the data rates of a specific flow or link workload statistics. In SDR, the controller can perform collection on the information about the gains of the wireless channels and the interference among the communication links [202]. Despite of the disadvantage of scalability – however can be alleviated by deploying the logically centralized control plane – SDN makes it possible to carry out traffic engineering globally – i.e., network-wide – and thereby to optimize network performance.

- SDN provides flexibility to control traffic and network behaviors. In the traffic engineering implementation using OpenFlow, packet flows can be identified according to the matching rules specified by network management applications. Thus, the granularity of data flows in performing TE can be adjusted dynamically. The concept of SDN also enables cross-layer management of networks, in which information from different layers serve as the basis for control decisions. For instance, the integration between SDR and SDN enables trade-off analyses for spectrum and flow coordination [35].

Following the guidelines introduced in Section 2.2.2, this book builds upon a SDN-assisted TE framework for network optimization, and it contains the elements shown in Figure 2.5.

In the general architecture of a SDN-based traffic engineering framework, a *SDN controller* is the bridging component that receives and relays network states and traffic engineering decisions [92]. Relying on interfaces obeying SDN standards, a controller communicates with underlying network devices to collect their operation states and send instructions to adjust their configurations. Meanwhile, a controller can also cooperate with other components, like a traffic monitor or an application coordinator to obtain more detailed information. To support the decision making process, the TE engine collects and aggregates these information and shares with a SDN controller.

A *TE engine* is the essential part that implements algorithms and strategies to carry out traffic engineering (e.g., schedule routing paths) as well as to compute configurations for network devices. The TE engine triggers the network reconfiguration based on *events* that reflect the changes of the network environment or states. Depending on the goals of traffic engineering, the triggering events are diverse. For instance, the TE engine performs flow scheduling to avoid network congestions upon the detection of large flows [67]. To conserve the power consumption of, the TE engine determines the on/off states of links and flow paths when it receives a Traffic Matrix (TM) [98].

While the SDN technology provides the limited functionality of network monitoring, a dedicated *network monitor* measuring and analyzing network performance and traffic workloads, is able to collect more detailed information. A network monitor can be a native controller application that only relies on interfaces defined in SDN standards [39]. It also can build upon existing monitoring solutions such as sFlow [190] and function as an independent element that communicates with the controller [205]. The important network performance parameters to assess the effectiveness of traffic engineering include the packet latency, flow throughput and link/port utilization [219]. Another important functionality of a network monitor is to continuously measure and analyze network traffic [198]. Depending on the timeliness of reported traffic information, a network monitor provides:

- Real-time flow statistics. This information reflects the current properties of traffic flows and a TE engine can *reactively* adjust network configurations.

- Predicted flow patterns. A network monitor not only collects flow statistics but also adopts analysis methods to understand the evolution of traffic workloads. The predicted traffic information enables a TE engine to *proactively* reconfigure a network.

A *network resource provisioner* is a conceptual component that informs a controller about network service requirements, such as demanded bandwidth, of communication entities. It is the job of a TE engine to accommodate the proposed resource demands, and at the same time to fulfill any objective of network optimization. In many cases, a network resource provisioner is a module or plugin of a cloud, big data or network management framework, rather than a standalone component. For instance, in multi-tenant cloud environment, a cloud controller accepts virtual machine requests from users. Besides the demands for the computation resources, these requests also contain QoS requirements on the connections among VMs [3, 16, 31]. In a SDN network management framework, such as Merlin [201], a network negotiator allows applications to declare their resource requirements in advance. As for cooperative big data analytical applications, a Transfer Controller (TC) is envisioned in the application layer to monitor and control the data transfers on the participating nodes [37, 38]. Consequently, in this case, a TC serves as a provisioner that has the knowledge of network resource demands.

## 2.3 CHALLENGES ON RESOURCE EFFICIENCY IN SDN

Improving the utilization efficiency of different types of resources in a network is crucial to achieve the purpose of network performance enhancement and Opex reduction. As described previously, the techniques of network softwarization enable dynamic operations of data forwarding, device management and network monitoring. Correspondingly, in a SDN-based network, there exist a data plane, a control plane and a monitoring plane. Each of these functional planes has its unique challenge in reducing or protecting their corresponding resources. This section introduces these challenges and their background information to assist understanding the rest chapters of this book. Additionally, by using toy examples, we show how SDN-assisted traffic engineering can be used to achieve network resource efficiency in different scenarios.

### 2.3.1 *Improving efficiency of bandwidth utilization in network monitoring plane*

Bandwidth is a crucially important resource in SDN, which is consumed by two types of flows: (i) application data flows exchanged among network users, and (ii) management data flows exchanged between network controllers and networking devices. Conserving the bandwidth consumed by application data flows can be done either by reducing the volume of generated data or reducing the distance between communication pairs. Joe et al. [110] propose to jointly consider the placement of Virtual Machine (VM) and routing to improve resource utilization defined as the combination of the network and host machine utilization. The formulated problem is solved by using the Markov approximation method.

In this book, we focus on improving efficiency of bandwidth consumption for network management, especially for network monitoring. As a result, in this subsection, we first introduce network monitoring for SDN and briefly discuss corresponding resource reduction opportunities. Next, we show how traffic engineering and cross-layer SDN configuration can help to reduce bandwidth consumption in a network monitoring system.

2.3.1.1 *Network monitoring and resource consumption*

Network monitoring has been an important topic in both academia and network industry for long time. Researchers and network device manufacturers have developed many efficient monitoring frameworks, such as SNMP, NetFlow and sFlow, to gain insights of network states. As the needs for customized dynamic network measurement increase in today's complex network architectures, monitoring frameworks rely on the functionalities provided by SDN and on so-called *software-defined measurement* [245]. Software-defined measurement architectures allow dynamic control over a network monitoring system, including: (i) flexible deployment of multiple monitoring tasks, (ii) coordination of monitoring locations, (iii) configuration of measurement timescales, and (iv) specification of monitoring targets [25, 158]. Performing measurement and monitoring consumes resources, such as processing resources, memory and bandwidth [157]. It is an important topic to design monitoring mechanisms with less resource consumption or achieve tradeoffs between resource consumption and measurement accuracy.

The procedure of network monitoring consists of collection, preprocessing, transmission, analysis and presentation [214]. Normally, analyzing and presenting monitoring data take place on a central machine or computing cluster that has no resource constraint. On the other hand, a control plane or monitoring plane consisting of networking devices is more sensitive to additional resource consumption. Thus, analysis and optimization of resource consumption usually takes place at the stages of collection, preprocessing and transmission. For instance, sketch-based approaches are proposed to efficiently collect network traffic information. Instead of obtaining statistics associated with each individual flow, sketch-based approaches, such as OpenSketch [245] and SCREAM [159], use hashing functions to compute and aggregate flow statistics, which leads to less memory consumption on programmable switches. Transmission of locally collected monitoring data causes bandwidth consumption. As SDN-based monitoring systems have a central architecture, a controller needs to communicate with local monitoring agents (e.g., switch software or hardware that inspects incoming packets to reconfigure monitoring strategies and obtain monitoring results). From the perspective of traffic engineering, scheduling the locations to capture primitive monitoring data as well as the routing paths to transport both monitored and monitoring data, is able to conserve the network resource, in particular valuable network bandwidth, during transmission of monitoring data.

2.3.1.2 *Conserving bandwidth for monitoring based on SDN and traffic engineering*

A simple operation, network flow counting, is fundamental to complex monitoring tasks such as detecting Heavy Hitters (HHs) carrying large volumes of data packets [237] and deriving Traffic Matrix (TM) representing data volumes between every original/destination pairs [94]. The OpenFlow protocol provides interfaces for a controller to send queries on traffic statistics and receive responses via two types of messages: (i) per-flow messages

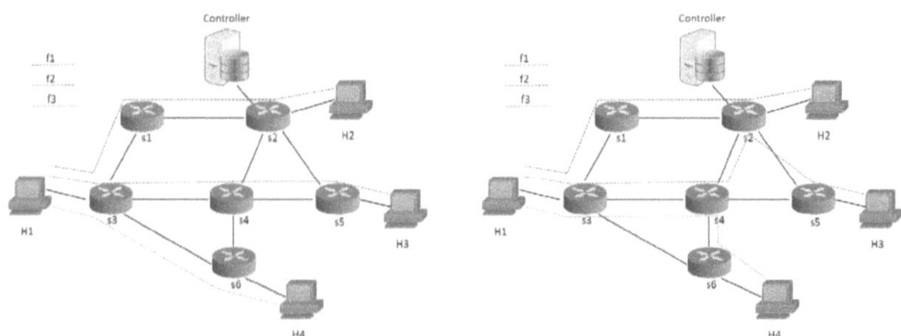

(a) Before using TE to optimize the cost of transmitting monitoring messages.　　(b) After using TE to optimize the cost of transmitting monitoring messages.

*Figure 2.6:* An example of reducing transmission cost in the monitoring plane using SDN-assisted TE, inspired by [204]. In this example, the network has four hosts and six switches. Three flows exist in the network: f1:H1 − H2, f2:H1 − H3, f3:H1 − H4. The monitoring controller is attached to s3.

(e.g., *ofp_flow_stats_request* and *ofp_flow_stats*), which contain a header and counter information of a single flow; (ii) aggregation messages (e.g., *ofp_aggregate_stats_request* and *ofp_aggregate_stats_reply*), which contain a header and counter information of flows passing through a same switch. Several existing approaches rely on TE to reduce the overhead of transmitting these messages [32, 204, 208]. The idea behind these approaches is to plan routing paths of the flows under monitoring, so that they can colocate at a switch. In this case, the controller uses aggregation messages as much as possible, since per-flow messages have a higher header overheads for the same amount of flows. We use an example to illustrate this basic idea. Figure 2.6 shows the set-up of a network, and a monitoring controller is attached to switch s2 and uses the in-band control method. In Figure 2.6a, the three flows (f1, f2 and f3) all follow the shortest paths in the network. However, this naive approach causes the monitoring controller to use per-flow messages to acquire flow counters for the flows. On the contrary, in Figure 2.6b, two flows are rerouted so that f2 passes s2 and the controller can use aggregation messages instead of per-flow ones to obtain flow counters. Meanwhile, f3 is pushed away from its shortest path to reduce the distance between its query switch and the controller (s3 $\rightarrow$ s1 $\rightarrow$ s2 vs. s4 $\rightarrow$ s2).

Monitoring systems relying on the interfaces defined in the OpenFlow protocols provide basic network measurement functionalities. More sophisticated monitoring applications, such as Deep Packet Inspection (DPI), allow comprehensive analyses on traffic flows. As the concept of NFV emerges, virtualized network monitoring agents (e.g., virtualized DPI) can be deployed flexibly in SDN networks and placed in the close proximity of switches [101]. Traffic flows are redirected or mirrored to the in-network monitoring agents for statistic collection and inspection. The aspect of reducing the cost of a NFV-based monitoring systems has attracted research attention [23, 47, 127]. Similar to the example presented in this subsection, the common approach is to jointly consider the resource consumption of deployed virtualized network monitors and the cost of rerouting data flows to them. In these approaches, the routing decisions of TE are part of the solution space.

### 2.3.2 *Improving efficiency of power consumption in the network forwarding plane*

As mentioned in Section 1, delivering data packets with less power consumption helps to reduce the operation cost of network owners and footprints of carbon emissions of ICT systems. To achieve the goal of reducing power consumption for networking, the following approaches have been presented in the literature [55, 216]: (i) re-engineering hardware used in networking devices to make them more energy-efficient [28]; (ii) offloading processing of background traffic and deactivate the end device [183]; (iii) adapting the link rate to local flow workloads [82]; (iv) scheduling unnecessary components to enter the sleeping mode [98]. Among these methods, sleep-scheduling approaches heavily rely on traffic engineering. There are two different approaches to perform sleep scheduling, namely *connection-oriented* and *traffic-oriented* approaches. We briefly introduce both of these approaches but focus on traffic-oriented approaches in the next subsection since it is more relevant to this book.

Connection-oriented approaches focus on selecting a set of active network components to ensure the connectivity among the hosts that have communication demands. Traffic engineering is used to reroute traffic flows through those selected network components. Matsuura *et al.* [148] proposed to use a Steiner Tree Based (STB) method to connect edge nodes with a minimum subgraph of the original network topology. The network components that do not belong to the constructed subgraph are put into sleeping mode so as to reduce the power consumption of a network. In the proposed three-phase construction algorithm, a Steiner tree is firstly created to connect all the edge nodes. Afterwards, the algorithm uses the computed subgraph to calculate the available paths among the edge nodes. In the final phase, the algorithm substitutes a calculated path that is excessively long with the shortest path that is added to the Steiner tree.

Traffic-oriented approaches take information about traffic flows into the design of sleep-scheduling mechanisms. Benefiting from the global view and TE capability of SDN, a network management system uses traffic engineering to plan the routes or transmission orders of traffic flows without violating their QoS requirements (e.g., avoid congestion) to pass through limited number of network components or to reduce the overall transmission time accordingly. Depending on whether a network component hosts traffic workloads, the scheduler configures operation states of network components.

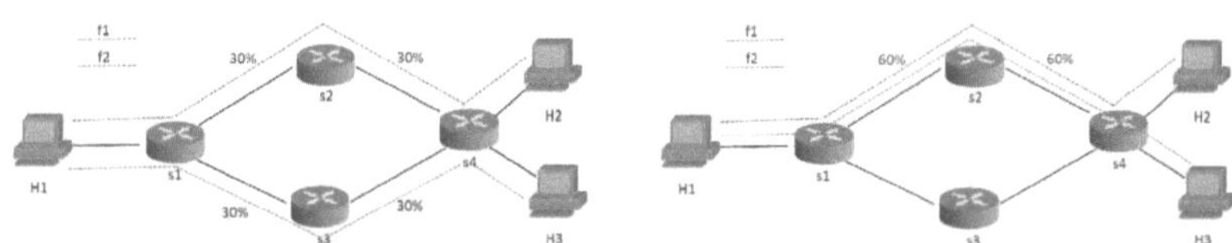

(a) Before using TE to optimize the link utilization and power consumption.

(b) After using TE to optimize the link utilization and power consumption.

*Figure 2.7:* An example of reducing power consumption in the data plane using SDN-assisted traffic engineering, inspired by [246]. In this example, the network has three hosts and four switches. Two flows exist in the network: f1:H1 − H2, f2:H1 − H3.

### 2.3.2.1 *Reducing power consumption based on SDN and traffic engineering*

Traffic-oriented approaches fall into two subcategories: *flow consolidation* and *flow scheduling*. Flow scheduling is based on exclusive routing that allocates all bandwidth of a link to only one flow, instead of the fair sharing policy used in flow consolidation. This method is able to further improve link utilization and speed up the transmission of a set of flows on *"non-bottleneck links"* [133]. In addition to achieving the power efficiency of SDN, flow scheduling uses flow deadline and completion time as secondary objectives, thus they are time domain approaches [234].

Flow consolidation [134] is a well-investigated traffic engineering method to improve the utilization of network components by aggregating data flows to a limited number of links. Colocated flows fairly share link bandwidth by enforcing rate limiting on each forwarding device. Figure 2.7 shows an example of flow consolidation. In Figure 2.7a, the flows, f1 and f2, follow the two paths in the network. Although each flow only consumes 30% of the link capacity, all network components are kept in the active mode to serve the traffic demands. On the contrary, in Figure 2.7a, these two flows are consolidated onto one path and the network links of the other path can be put into sleeping mode.

In the early stage of the development of SDN, ElasticTree [98] is proposed to improve the power efficiency in SDN-based DCN. This system consists of three logical modules, namely optimizer, routing and power control. ElasticTree takes traffic matrices, network topology and a power model for each switch as the inputs. It also employs three different types of algorithms (formal model based on the multi-commodity flow problem, greedy bin-packing and topology-aware heuristic) to compute the *"optimal network subset"*. GreenTE provides the detailed formulation on the selection of routing so as to *"maximize the power saving from turning off line-cards as well as satisfying performance constraints including link utilization and packet delay"* [246]. The contribution of GreenTE also includes a practical heuristic algorithm that only uses limited searching space of solutions. Wang et al. [225] model the power-efficient TE with similar formulation, and propose to use an AI model,

Blocking Island Paradigm, to quickly find the power-saving configurations for SDN-based DCN. Several work also considers performing energy-efficient TE under other types of constraints. In addition to the widely used heuristic algorithms and formal model based on the optimization theory, Zhang et al. [251] propose to use game theory to model the balance between the power efficiency and link workload balancing. Lin et al. [138] consider the negative impacts of energy-aware traffic engineering: activating only a subset of network components reduces path diversities in a network. Thus, they propose models and algorithms that integrates terminal reliability and route reliability.

Chapter 4 in this book addresses a resource efficiency problem for a SDN network that contains heterogeneous communication media as introduced in Section 2.1.2.2. More specifically, this book investigates how to reduce power consumption for a SDN-based data center network that consists of both wired and directional wireless communication links. Reducing power consumption for such hybrid SDN networks remains unexplored due to the fact that the integration of OpenFlow-based SDN and hardware component management starts only very recently and are not yet widely deployed. However, the basic idea to reduce power consumption in Ethernet-based networks by powering off unused components is still valid when considering newly emerged constraints in this type of SDN.

### 2.3.3 *Mitigating abusive usage of resources in the network control plane*

This book relies on the principle of SDN to design models and algorithms that improve the resource efficiency of computer networks. The previous subsections discussed the benefits brought by using SDN to manage a network. Although SDN utilizes the overview of a network to make global decisions, its centralized architecture naturally has the disadvantage that a network controller may become the bottleneck to respond to large volumes of control messages. Significant research efforts have been devoted to the improvement of the SDN control plane regarding its scalability and availability. As it is surveyed in [17], SDN controller frameworks implementing distributed control planes, either in the flat or hierarchical architecture, are capable of reducing the workload of a single controller and achieving control plane resilience. However, in a network resource management system that relies on SDN to perform scheduling, the existence of malicious network entities can disrupt its operation by abusing the control plane resource that is required to comply with the management tasks.

### 2.3.3.1 *Denial-of-Service attacks on the control plane*

The security of the SDN control plane may be affected mainly by the following threats: (i) Denial-of-Service attacks, (ii) unauthorized access to the control plane, and (iii) malicious controller applications sending invalid control messages [5, 189]. Among these potential security concerns for the SDN controller, DoS attacks are identified as *"the most threatening*

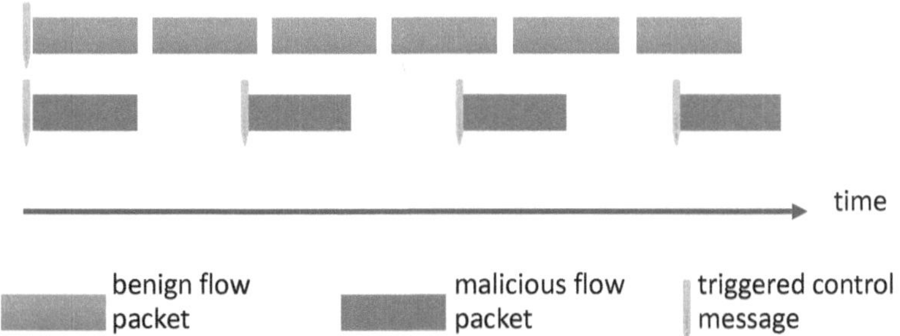



*Figure 2.8:* An example to show the principle of DoS attacks on the SDN control plane. In each benign flow, only the first packet triggers a control message. In each malicious flow, every packet can trigger a control message due to its large inter-arrival time of packets.

*security challenges"* [5]. The purpose of DoS attacks is to deplete control plane resource so that the communication requests from legitimate network users and other management tasks cannot be fulfilled in time. Thus, DoS attacks that target on the SDN control plane can be also called *Control Plane Saturation* attacks. Due to the widely deployed OpenFlow-based SDN, DoS attacks exploring the vulnerability of the OpenFlow protocol receive significant attention. The resources of the control plane that are most exposed to such attacks include: storage space of the flow table in OpenFlow switches, CPU of the hosting server running a SDN controller and control plane bandwidth used to transmit control messages [112].

The mechanism of DoS attacks to the SDN control plane is based on the process of handling communication requests from hosts as described in Section 2.1.1. The basic principle to saturate the control plane is to generate a large number of flow packets that will not match any flow rule in the flow tables of the receiving switches. Figure 2.8 illustrates this DoS attack principle. In OpenFlow, each installed flow rule has a *timeout* field specifying the maximum amount of hard time or idle time before the rule is removed. As a consequence, each unmatched flow packet results in two control packets: (i) `packet_in` message sent from the switch to the controller and (ii) `ofp_flow_mod` or `packet_out` messages sent in the opposite direction. Floods of these control packets, in turn, result in consuming the computational resources of the controller [224] as well as the control plane bandwidth. Subsequently, the legitimate flow packets will be either dropped or delayed [194].

The effectiveness of abusive usage of control plane resources mainly depends on the information collected by the adversary, about the network and the applied flow rules, during the so-called network fingerprinting [194]. For instance, if the adversary learns that the packet matching criteria depend on the destination IP address, an effective attack strategy would be to rapidly generate a large number of flow packets with different destination IPs. Additionally, the adversary can amplify the attack if it also knows the expiry times of flow rules. It can use these information to generate the flow packets so that they always arrive shortly after the corresponding flow rule's timeout.

Traffic engineering, including flow packet reshaping and flow path planning, is one class of methods to counter abusive resource usage in the SDN network control plane. There are several frameworks that implement a protection module on the controller side to prevent Control Plane Saturation (CPS) attacks. Rajat et al. [112] discuss two types of DoS attacks in SDN. One type of DoS attacks targets the flow tables while the other one targets the control plane bandwidth. Their evaluation shows that saturating the flow tables and the control plane result in dropping legitimate flow packets. As a mitigation approach, they suggest to limit the rate of flow packets using the SDN meter table.

FloodDefender [191] is a network control framework for protecting the resources in the data and control planes. The approach used by FloodDefender to mitigate abusive usage of control plane resource is to offload traffic from a switch to its neighboring switches. FloodDefender also implements a packet filtering module in the controller to identify malicious flows based on the arrival rates of packet_in messages.

SDN-Guard [61] is a controller application that manages the flow packets according to the information it receives from an intrusion detection system. This information includes the threat probability of each flow. SDN-Guard reroutes potentially malicious flow packets through the least utilized links. In addition, as a proactive action, it assigns the flow rules a large hard timeout. Similar to SDN-Guard, FlowRanger [227] uses a trust management system to prioritize the incoming packet_in messages, and stores them in a queue. The higher the priority of the message the faster it will delivered to other controller modules, like a routing module.

SECO [224] is another controller-based solution. It uses a threshold based on statistics of the switch ports and controller's CPU utilization. In the controller, SECO drops all unmatched packets arriving from a switch port if the connected hosts are compromised. It also ignores all control packets arriving from switches out of control.

Due to the delays existing in the control plane, transmitting and analyzing all incoming control messages on the controller side could lead to delayed detection. To cope with this problem, in Chapter 6, we develop a mitigation method, which operates alongside packet forwarding devices, to reduce the additional resource consumption of generating and transmitting a large volumes of control messages as early as possible.

## 2.3.4 *Summary*

In this chapter, we provided necessary background knowledge to understand the scenarios and assumptions in the following presented contributions. In particular, Section 2.1 introduced the concept of software defined networking, and its extensions to realize cross-layer control in the network. Such a cross-layer approach is a fundamental in this book to not only perform traffic engineering by manipulating flow paths but also to control behavior of elements in other layers, such as the location to deploy a piece of software or the operation status of hardware. Section 2.2 discussed the history and concept of SDN-assisted traffic engineering. Lastly, we discussed three challenges in reducing resource consumption in the data plane, monitoring plane and control plane of SDN, and existing approaches to tackle them.

# CHAPTER 3

# RESOURCE-EFFICIENT NETWORK MONITORING

A monitoring system plays an important role in network management because of its capability of performing analyses of traffic data, as explained in Section 2.2.3. In this chapter, we consider a monitoring system that provides the in-depth knowledge of packets: *per-packet based flow monitoring*. In this method, all or part of data packets belonging to a flow are examined locally by an additional module of a networking device or remotely on a dedicated machine. The information extracted from examined packets can be used to achieve simple tasks (e.g., flow counting) and complex tasks (e.g., diagnosing network performance issues [93]). In addition, security services, such as hostile traffic identification [121, 143], intrusion detection systems and application-level fingerprinting demand thorough examination of network packets [154, 243].

The SDN-based packet monitoring systems proposed in [196] and [162] allow switches or routers to duplicate *original data flows* on a per-packet basis, according to the dynamically configured matching fields of data flows. The *mirrored data flows* are sent to flow monitors for analyses by predefined algorithms. The separation between the original data flows and the mirrored data flows (i.e., between the network's *data plane* and *monitoring plane*) is a common practice in network monitoring [12, 33]. It brings benefits to the overall performance and reliability of the monitoring system. For example, the congestion in the data plane will not affect the transmission of mirrored data flows in the monitoring plane, and vice versa [64].

The aforementioned separation can be achieved either physically or virtually. Original and mirrored data flows in the physical separation approach traverse through isolated network channels built upon different underlying communication technologies. For example, in hybrid data center networks consisting of both 60 GHz wireless links and wired optical fiber links [88, 91], the wireless links and the wired links can be dedicated to the mirrored data flows and to the original data flows, respectively. Due to the different energy consumption profiles of these two communication technologies, the resources required to transmit the original data flows and those required to transmit the mirrored data flows are different [74, 215]. At the same time, the virtual separation approach relies on the state-of-the-art network slicing technology [85, 193]. This technology allows to allocate exclusive slices of network resources to the original data flows and mirrored data flows. Depending on the QoS requirements of the allocated network slices, techniques like Dynamic Voltage and Frequency Scaling can be used to change the execution rates of the Network Processor

Unit (NPU) allocated to the network slice [14]. In this case, it also costs different amounts of resources to transmit original and mirrored data flows in the distinct communication planes. The common practice to quantify such differences is to multiply the bandwidth consumption with a weighted value.

Several existing approaches have addressed the problem of reducing the network resource consumption of the monitoring plane by stretching the path length of original data flows [32, 204, 208]. One of the negative consequences of the the existing work is that the network resource consumption of original data flows increases correspondingly, which also contributes to the transmission cost in a network. To address this problem, we present REMO, a **R**esource **E**fficient distributed **MO**nitoring system in this chapter. REMO is a general framework that optimizes the global resource consumption caused by the transmission of original and mirrored data flows in isolated communication planes. REMO achieves this goal by employing a two-step scheduling approach: Firstly, REMO places the flow monitors at central places in the network, so that the mirrored data flows do not need to traverse long paths from the switch to the flow monitor. Secondly, in order to further reduce resource consumption, REMO leverages the data path programmability provided by SDN. It carefully selects the paths (either one of the shortest paths or a stretched one) for the original data flows to redirect them even closer to the flow monitors.

We use an Integer Linear Programming (ILP) model to optimize the flow monitor placement, and a Mixed Integer Linear Programming (MILP) model to optimize paths to embed original flows and the selection of switches to duplicate flows. More precisely, planning placement of the flow monitors determines the location to run an instance of the flow monitor. The result of flow embedding chooses the paths that original data flows should traverse. As for the result of mirroring switch selection, it determines which switches should duplicate flows. Furthermore, to overcome the complexity of directly solving the formulated MILP problem, we propose a heuristic algorithm to efficiently solve the problem.

We evaluate the performance of REMO – i.e. its ability to reduce the costs of transmitting original and mirrored data flows – through extensive numerical simulations. Furthermore, we compare REMO with several baseline strategies. Overall, the results show that REMO is effective in reducing the overall communication cost. Compared with baseline strategies, REMO is able to save over 50% of the network resource consumption, when transmission in the monitoring plane is more expensive. Our results also show that increasing the number of flow monitors can reduce overall resource consumption of at least 10% compared with the case where only one flow monitor exists.

The remainder of this chapter is organized as follows: Section 3.1 describes the setups of the envisioned packet-based monitoring system, as well as a motivation example to illustrate the basic idea of optimizing its global network resource consumption. Section 3.2 introduces the formal model to solve this problem and Section 3.3 presents a heuristic algorithm that has near-optimal performance. The proposed model and algorithm are evaluated in Section 3.4. We provide more background and related work in Section 3.5 and conclude this contribution in Section 3.6.

## 3.1 SYSTEM SETUPS AND A MOTIVATING EXAMPLE

Compared with traditional sampling techniques, such as sFlow [190], that performs per-port/per-interface sampling, the SDN-based approach is able to perform sampling on a per-flow basis to achieve better flexibility and granularity of the packet sampling strategies. Integrating the flow packet sampling capacity into SDN can be currently implemented in two approaches. The first approach is directly modify the implementation code of the SDN switches, for example, Open vSwitch. Philip et al. [229] propose to extend the OpenFlow protocol with the sampling support so as to unveil individual flows behind a wildcard flow entry. In [243], the coordination algorithm selects a few SDN switches to perform sampling on all passing flows to detect malicious packets. However, sampling all passing flows on the SDN switches can generate redundant sampled packets, because multiple SDN switches on the path of one flow can be chosen as the sampling switches. FleXam [196] is a more flexible per-flow sampling extension enabling network security applications such as the port scan attack detection. This extension allows to control the sampling rate, the field of packets to be sampled and where the sampled packets should be propagated.

In order to perform per-packet based traffic analysis, in this chapter, we consider a distributed flow monitoring system relying on switches that can duplicate packets of selected data flows. There are several flow monitors deployed in the network and attached to the switches. Each switch is associated with one of the flow monitors. That is, a switch transmits all of its mirrored flow packets over the shortest path in the isolated monitoring plane to the same flow monitor. Besides, we assume that a (logically) centralized network monitoring coordinator continuously collects link cost information for both the monitoring and data planes. It computes the placement of flow monitors, and places the flow monitor instances on the desired locations in the network. The coordinator also obtains the global knowledge about the flows under monitoring, before or during the transmission of flows. The first case happens when a coflow exists. Coflow is a collection of parallel flows among hosts, occurring during the intermediate stages of big data applications [38]. The flow information can be known in advance by the network coordinator, through its channel with a data migration scheduler [174]. The second case happens when the network coordinator is notified that the flow bandwidth requirements change. Then the coordinator is responsible for calculating the paths for original data flows, as well as selecting the switches to duplicate them.

Our goal is to reduce the overall consumption of network resources used for transmitting both original and mirrored data flows. As mentioned in the introduction, we assume that transmission of mirrored data flows (in the monitoring plane) and transmission of original

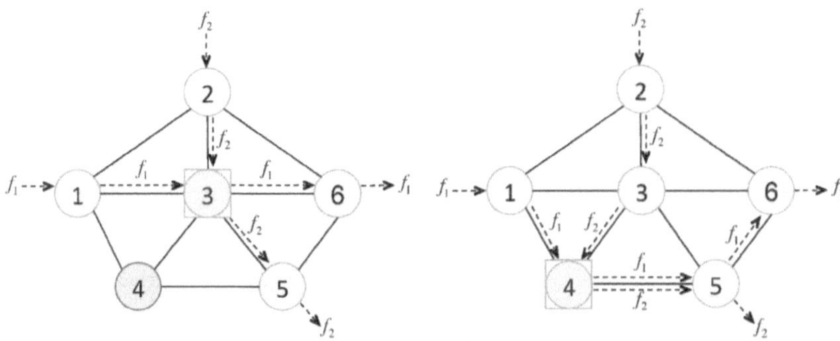

(a) The flow monitor is attached to Switch 3. $f_1$ and $f_2$ are embedded to the links using the shortest path algorithm.

(b) The flow monitor is attached to Switch 4. $f_1$ and $f_2$ are embedded to the links so as to force them to go through Switch 4.

*Figure 3.1:* Illustrative examples to show the overall network resource consumption is affected by the placement of flow monitors, the routing paths and flows mirroring locations.

data flows (in the data plane) possibly are associated different costs due to the transmission in different network channels or slices. We use toy examples shown in Figure 3.1 to motivate our work as well as to illustrate the problem which we aim to solve. We assume that the cost of transmitting a packet over one hop is 1 unit in the data plane and 5 units in the monitoring plane.

In Figure 3.1a, the flows $f_1$ and $f_2$ have the ingress/egress switch pairs $< 1,6 >$ and $< 2,5 >$, respectively. They follow the shortest paths. In this scenario, the minimum cost of network resource consumption of 4 units (including 4 units in the data plane, and 0 unit in the monitoring plane) is achieved by attaching the flow monitor to Switch 3, and also mirroring the two flows on Switch 3. Attaching the flow monitor to Switch 4, while keeping flow mirroring on Switch 3, increases the cost to 14 units (4 units in the data plane, and 10 units in the monitoring plane). In Figure 3.1b, we assume that the flow monitor is attached to Switch 4. If the flows $f_1$ and $f_2$ do not follow the shortest path anymore, but are embedded to the paths that contain Switch 4, the overall network resource consumption can be reduced from 14 units to 6 units (6 units in the data plane, and 0 unit in the monitoring plane).

To conclude, the overall network resource consumption is affected by the placement of flow monitors, the routing paths and locations to mirror flows. The monitoring coordinator is responsible for making three decisions: (i) where to place the flow monitors, (ii) which path the original data flows should traverse and (iii) which switch(es) should mirror data flows and later transmit the mirrored flows to the corresponding monitors.

| Variable | Definition |
| --- | --- |
| $V$ | set of switches in the network topology |
| $E$ | set of links in the network topology |
| $D_{u,m}$ | the distance (measured in hops) of the shortest path from switch $u$ to switch $m$ |
| $R^m, R^d$ | the cost to transmit data flows over one hop in the monitoring plane and in the data plane, respectively |
| $i :< s_i, d_i, b_i >$ | flow info containing ingress switch $s_i$, egress switch $d_i$ and the bandwidth consumption $b_i$ |
| $c_m$ | binary, whether to connect a controller to switch $m$ |
| $a_{u,m}$ | binary, whether switch $u$ is associated with a flow monitor connected to switch $m$ |
| $w_i^{u,v}$ | binary, whether to embed a flow $i$ into the link $u, v$ |
| $t_i^u$ | binary, whether a flow is mirrored on the switch $u$ |
| $p_i^{u,v}$ | continuous, voltage value on the link $u, v$ for the flow $i$ |
| $q_i^u$ | binary, whether the flow $i$ passes the switch $u$ |
| $B$ | the bandwidth capacity of a link |
| $L_i$ | the shortest path length computed for the flow $i$ |

*Table 3.1:* Variables used in the optimization model and heuristic algorithm of REMO.

## 3.2 FORMAL MODEL DESCRIPTION

In this subsection, we introduce our formulation that reduces the overall network resource consumption. The model consists of two consecutive steps: (i) *Flow Monitor Placement and Switch Binding (FMPSB)* and (ii) *Flow Embedding and Mirroring Switch Selection (FEMSS)*. FMPSB depends on the topology of the underlying network, and it takes place when the network topology evolves or the number of flow monitors changes. FEMSS takes as input the result of the flow monitor placement step and information about a batch of flows, including their ingress/egress switches and current bandwidth consumption.

It is also possible to jointly compute FMPSB and FEMSS and perform flow monitor placement and flow scheduling after the flow information is obtained [186]. However, we argue that it is preferable to compute flow monitor placement without prior knowledge about the data flows, to avoid frequent migration of the flow monitors.

The network topology that we consider can be represented as a graph $G = (V, E)$, where $V$ is the set of switches being capable of mirroring flow packets, and $E$ is the set of links connecting them. We use $k$ to denote the number of flow monitors that need to be placed, and $m \in V$ to represent a potential switch to attach a flow monitor. Table 4.1 lists the variables used in the model.

We detail the models to solve FMPSB and FEMSS in Section 3.2.1 and Section 3.2.2, respectively.

### 3.2.1 *Flow monitor placement and switch binding*

The main goal of the FMPSB step is to achieve the lowest average distance between switches and monitors in the monitoring plane, without the knowledge of the flow pattern. In the following object function, $a_{u,m}$ is a binary variable that indicates whether a switch $u$ is associated with a flow monitor connected to switch $m$. $D_{u,m}$ represents the distance between of the shortest path from switch $u$ to switch $m$, which is measured in the number of hops.

$$\min \frac{1}{|V|} \sum_{u \in V, m \in V} a_{u,m} \cdot D_{u,m} \tag{3.1}$$

**Monitor placement constraints:**

$$\sum_{m \in V} c_m = k \tag{3.2}$$

$$\sum_{u \in V} a_{u,m} \leqslant |V| \cdot c_m, \text{ for } m \in V \tag{3.3}$$

$$\sum_{m \in V} a_{u,m} = 1, \text{ for } u \in V \tag{3.4}$$

Constraint (3.2) indicates that the total number of flow monitors that needs to be placed is equal to $k$. Constraint (3.3) states that switches use a switch $m$ as the destination for mirrored flows only if that switch is attached with a flow monitor ($c_m = 1$). For simplicity of configuration in the monitoring plane, we use Constraint (3.4) to show that a switch has only one binded flow monitor and the mirrored data flows from the same switch are sent to that particular binded flow monitor.

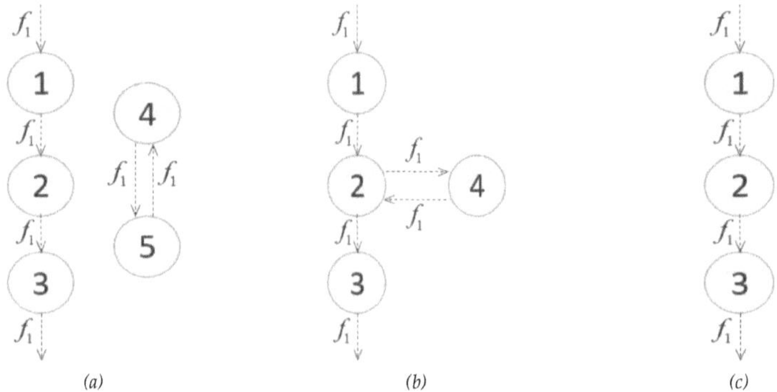

*Figure 3.2:* Steps to generate a simple path containing no loops: (a) Flow path with disjoint paths; (b) Non-simple path with cycles after using the method proposed in [32]; (c) Simple path after removing the attached cycles.

### 3.2.2 *Flow embedding and mirroring switch selection*

The goal of the FEMSS step is to optimize the paths to embed original data flows as well as the selection of mirroring switches. The objective is to minimize the total resource consumption of transmitting mirrored data flows in the monitoring plane – represented by the first part of Equation (3.5) – and that of transmitting original data flows in the data plane – represented by the second part of Equation (3.5). In the following objective function, $R^m$ and $R^d$ represent the corresponding cost per data rate to transmit data flows over one hop in the monitoring plane and in the data plane. $t_i^u$ is a decision variable indicating whether a flow $i$ is mirrored on the switch $u$. The location of a flow monitor, which is indicated by $c_m$, is a known variable computed in the FMPSB step. It is important to note that the mirrored data flows in the monitoring plane follow the shortest path from the switch to the flow monitor. In addition, we use $w_i^{u,v}$ to present the selection of the path for the original data flow.

$$\min R^m \sum_u \sum_m \sum_i t_i^u \cdot c_m \cdot D_{u,m} \cdot b_i + R^d \sum_{(u,v)} \sum_i w_i^{u,v} \cdot b_i \tag{3.5}$$

**Flow conservation constraints:**

$$\sum_{v \in neighbor(u)} w_i^{u,v} - \sum_{v \in neighbor(u)} w_i^{v,u} = \begin{cases} 1, u = s_i \\ -1, u = d_i \\ 0, otherwise \end{cases} \tag{3.6}$$

Constraint (3.6) forces the standard flow conservation rule in which a flow must leave a non-ingress/egress switch, if that flow passes through it.

**Simple path constraints:**

$$p_i^{u,v} \leqslant w_i^{u,v}, \text{ for all } i \tag{3.7}$$

$$\alpha q_i^u \leqslant \begin{cases} 1 + \sum_{(u,v)}(p_i^{u,v} - p_i^{v,u}) & u = d_i \\ \sum_{(u,v)}(p_i^{u,v} - p_i^{v,u}) & otherwise \end{cases} \tag{3.8}$$

$$q_i^u \geqslant (w_i^{u,v} + w_i^{v,u})/2 \tag{3.9}$$

The flow conservation constraint is not sufficient to remove disjoint paths. Figure 3.2a shows such a disjoint path. Therefore, we use the voltage value based method proposed in [32] to remove the disjoint paths. In that method, each link traversed by a flow has a continuous voltage value $p_i^{u,v}$ indicated by Constraint (3.7). $q_i^u$ indicates whether a flow $i$ passes the switch $u$. In Constraint (3.8), $\alpha$ is a small value (less than $1/|E|$), and the voltage value of the outgoing link must be larger than that of the incoming link. The idea behind this constraint is that a flow must always follow the direction in which the voltage value on the link increases. Constraint (3.9) guarantees that $q_i^u$ is 1 only if a flow $i$ passes a link that has the end point $u$.

The generated non-simple path containing the cycles, as shown in Figure 3.2b, is a valid solution in [32]. However, the flow traffic still has to traverse attached cyclic links, which leads to additional bandwidth consumption in the data plane. Thus, we use Constraint (3.10) to further remove attached cyclic links and generate only simple paths as shown in Figure 3.2c.

$$\sum_{(u,v) \in E} w_i^{u,v} \leqslant 1, \text{ for } u \neq d_i \tag{3.10}$$

**Mirroring switch constraints:**

$$t_i^u \leqslant q_i^u, \text{ for all } i \tag{3.11}$$

$$\sum_{u} t_i^u = 1, \text{ for all } i \tag{3.12}$$

Constraint (3.11) and Constraint (3.12) imply that only one switch belonging to the path of the original data flow can duplicate its packets.

**Data plane bandwidth and path length constraints:**

To avoid congestion in the data plane, Constraint (3.13) indicates that the aggregated bandwidth consumption on a data plane link should not exceed its capacity. Recall that we can stretch the paths of original data flows to decrease the overall resource consumption, when it costs more to transmit mirrored data flows in the monitoring plane than in the data plane. However, stretching the paths of original data flows means that the original data flow paths can be longer than their shortest paths. Thus, instead of aggressively pushing original data flows closer to the flow monitors, we take their path length into consideration and enforce an upper limit on it using Constraint (3.14). In this constraint, $\beta$ is the path length stretch ratio, which is defined, for a flow $i$, as the ratio of the maximum allowed path length to the shortest path length $L_i$.

$$\sum_{(u,v)\in E} b_i w_i^{u,v} \leqslant B \tag{3.13}$$

$$\sum_{(u,v)\in E} w_i^{u,v} \leqslant \beta L_i, \text{ for all } (u,v) \tag{3.14}$$

## 3.3 NEAR-OPTIMAL HEURISTIC ALGORITHM

The MILP formulation for flow embedding and mirroring switch selection, which we presented in Section 3.2, is NP-Hard. Thus, solving it using an optimizer requires a considerable amount of time on a regular desktop machine, ranging from several seconds to hours depending on the problem size. To cope with this problem, we develop a heuristic algorithm that provides a near-optimal performance for the formulated MILP and drastically reduces computation time.

We find experimentally that solving the current formulated ILP for the FMPSB subproblem only costs a dosen of milliseconds, even for a large-sized network. More importantly, the FMPSB step takes place only when the network topology changes. On the contrary, directly solving the MILP formulation for the FEMSS subproblem is a more complex task, which is unsuitable for large-sized networks with many flows. Thus, we design a heuristic algorithm,

---

**Algorithm 1** Heuristic FEMSS: Main Procedure

---

**Input:** a batch of monitored flows $F$ containing $f_i :< s_i, r_i, v_i >$, the flow monitor placement results

**Output:** the paths for original data flows and the switches to mirror them

**Main procedure:**

1: $A = \phi$
2: **for** $f_i$ in $F$ **do**
3:     $R = \phi$
4:     $L_{f_i}^{max} = \beta L_{f_i}^{shortest}$
5:     **for** each $m_j$ in $M$ **do**
6:        Using [240], find all the shortest paths $\{p_{f_i}^1, p_{f_i}^2, ...\}$ with length $n_j$, from ingress($f_i$) to switch($m_j$)
7:        **for** index in $n_j, n_j - 1, .., 0$ **do**
8:          **for** each path $p$ in $\{p_{f_i}^1, p_{f_i}^2, ...\}$ **do**
9:            switch $= p[index]$
10:            **if** switch is not bound with $m_j$ **then**
11:              continue
12:            **end if**
13:            $(s, r) = \text{SearchPath}(f_i, \text{switch}, p, L_f^{max})$
14:            **if** $(s, r) ==$ None **then**
15:              continue
16:            **else**
17:              $R = R \cup (f_i, s, r)$
18:            **end if**
19:          **end for**
20:          index=index-1
21:        **end for**
22:      **end for**
23:     From $R$, pick up $(f_i, s\prime, r\prime)$ leading to the minimum network resource consumption
24:     $A = A \cup (f_i, s\prime, r\prime)$
25: **end for**
26: **return** $A$

---

inspired by the deflection technique proposed in [166], to embed original data flows and select the switches to mirror their packets for the FEMSS subproblem.

Our heuristic algorithm utilizes the shortest paths among the network switches. The main idea is to iterate through the switches on the shortest paths from the flow ingress switch to the flow monitors, and use the shortest path from the iterated switches to the flow egress switch as the remaining path for a original data flow. Then, the procedure chooses the switch and its associated path that causes the minimum communication resource consumption, as its mirroring switch and the original data flow path correspondingly.

---

**Algorithm 2** SearchPath($f_i$, switch, p, $L_f^{max}$)

---

    **if** no link on path p is congested **then**
        find all the shortest paths $\{q_{f_i}^1, q_{f_i}^2, ...\}$ from switch to egress($f_i$)
        **for** each path q in $\{q_{f_i}^1, q_{f_i}^2, ...\}$ **do**
            **if** no link on path q is congested **and** $r = p \cup q$ is a simple path as in Figure 3.2c
    and $|r| \leqslant L_f^{max}$ **then**
                **return** (switch, r)
            **end if**
        **end for**
    **end if**
    **return** None

---

As shown in Algorithm 4, the procedure firstly identifies the shortest paths from the ingress switch of a flow to all the switches attached with a flow monitor (line: 6). Then, the procedure inspects each switch on the identified shortest paths to check whether it can be used to duplicate the flow packets. The inspection starts from the closest switches to the flow monitors (lines: 7 – 22). If one switch is not associated with the current flow monitor, the algorithm moves to the next one (lines: 10 – 12).

The SearchPath function, as shown in Algorithm 3, checks the status of the current path from the ingress switch to the potential mirroring switch, and rejects it if the path is congested. Afterwards, the algorithm starts searching the shortest path from the potential mirroring switch to the flow egress switch. A path gets accepted if it can form a complete data flow path without loops, and at the same time does not exceed the maximum path length constraint.

At the end of the main procedure in Algorithm 4, the mirroring switch and the path of original data flow leading to the minimum network resource consumption are selected as the final scheduling result for the flow.

## 3.4 EVALUATION

In this section, we report the evaluation of the above described models and heuristic algorithm for computing a resource efficient monitoring strategy. The evaluation is based on extensive numerical simulations. In Section 3.4.1, we describe the evaluation setup. In Section 3.4.2, we introduce the system performance metrics and parameters. Lastly, we present and discuss the results in Section 3.4.3.

### 3.4.1 *Setup*

We experiment with a synthetic network generated by FNSS [185], a widely used simulator in the networking community. The network contains 70 switches, and similar to the configuration in [23], its topology follows the Barabási-Albert model [18]. In addition, we randomly generate 500 original data flows being abstracted as ingress/egress switch pairs and data rates. The data rates follow the standard log-normal distribution to approximate the measured network traffic [8], with a mean value of 10 Mbps and a variance of 0.8 Mbps. We execute the simulations on a machine equipped with a Intel (R) Core (TM) i5-6500 CPU with four cores and 32GB RAM. We use Gurobi [84] as the optimization solver and repeat each experiment ten times.

### 3.4.2 *Evaluation metrics and focused parameters*

We use two system performance metrics: (i) the consumed network resources, and (ii) the path length of original data flows. The first metric allows us to evaluate the benefits gained by our solution in terms of reduction in the total resource consumption, which is caused by transmission of both original and mirrored data flows. The second metric indicates the penalty brought by our solution, in terms of the change of the path length experienced by original data flows.

In addition, we investigate the impact of the following three parameters on the system performance metrics.

- *Number of flow monitors:* It indicates how many flow monitors the monitoring system can utilize. The assumption is that more flow monitors can further reduce the total amount of resources consumed by the transmission of data flows. In the current design of REMO, the number of flow monitors is a given parameter to the system. Its value depends on the planned resource budget allocated to perform packet analysis.

- *Path length stretch ratio:* It is defined as the ratio of the maximum allowed path length to the shortest path length. This parameter is unique in our system since REMO incorporates the negative impact on the transmission in the data plane, such as longer routing paths, into the model. The assumption is that the larger this value the lower the relative resource consumption for transmitting the mirrored and original data flows.

- *Link cost ratio:* It is defined as the ratio of the cost of transmission in the monitoring plane to the cost of transmission in the data plane. This parameter intends to capture the relation between the possibly various communication cost, which is caused by using different transmission medium or network slices, in the data plane and monitoring plane. The assumption is that our solutions stretches the original data flow paths to reduce the resource consumption when this value is greater than 1.

### 3.4.3 Results

We report and discuss experiment results in this section.

#### 3.4.3.1 Impact of the path length stretch ratio and link cost ratio

In order to constraint the impact of the number of flow monitors, we fix the number of flow monitors to 2, and vary the path length stretch value by selecting it from the discrete value set $\{1, 1.5, 2, 3\}$. The link cost ratio between the monitoring plane and the data plane is chosen from the discrete value set $\{1, 2, 5\}$. It is worthy of noting that these values are synthetic to describe the relations of requirements and properties of a network, such as the actual communication cost in the data plane and monitoring plane.

Figure 3.3 depicts the impact of the path length stretch ratio and the link cost ratio on the resource consumption. In each subfigure, the network resource consumption is normalized by the obtained optimal result when the path length stretch ratio is 1. As shown in Figure 3.3b and Figure 3.3c, when the bandwidth cost per hop of the monitoring plane is greater than that of the data plane, increasing the path length stretch ratio helps reducing the overall network resource consumption caused by transmission of the original and mirrored data flows. More specifically, in the scenario where the link cost ratio is larger, our model and algorithm tend to further push the original data flows closer to the flow monitors to save more resources. For example, allowing the path length of the original data flows to be 0.5 longer than the shortest path, can reduce 30% of the network resource consumption when the link cost ratio is 5, compared with 10% resource reduction when the link cost ratio is 2. In addition, we can also see that our heuristic algorithm achieves near-optimal performance, except incurring more resource consumption when the path stretch ratio is 1. It is because that, in this case, the proposed heuristic algorithm may not select the optimal location to mirror data flows.

Figure 3.4 depicts the impact of the path stretch ratio and the link cost ratio on the computed path length of original data flows. As shown in Figure 3.4b and Figure 3.4c,

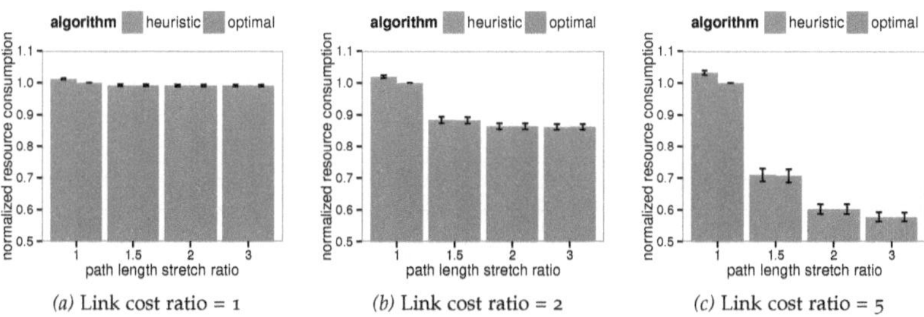

(a) Link cost ratio = 1  (b) Link cost ratio = 2  (c) Link cost ratio = 5

*Figure 3.3:* Impact of the path length stretch ratio and the link cost ratio on the resource consumption

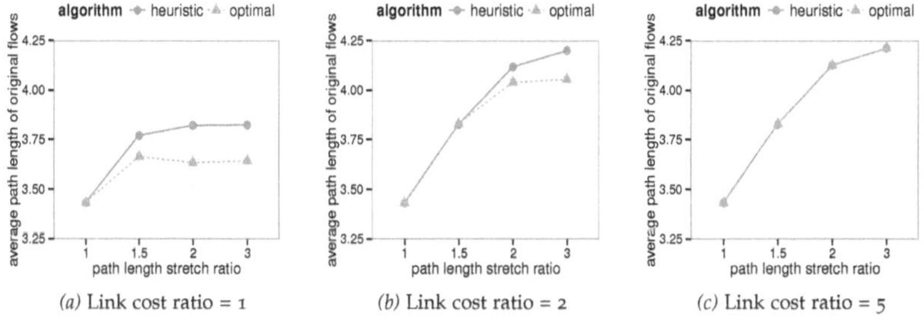

(a) Link cost ratio = 1  (b) Link cost ratio = 2  (c) Link cost ratio = 5

*Figure 3.4:* Impact of the path length stretch ratio and the link cost ratio on the path length of original data flows

increasing the path stretch ratio allows to divert the original data flows away from their shortest paths. We can also see that our model and algorithm push the original data flows more towards the flow monitors when the link cost ratio increases. For example, increasing the path length stretch ratio from 2 to 3 cannot further reduce resource consumption through path stretching when the link cost ratio is 1 or 2. Our heuristic algorithm generates slightly longer paths for original data flows. This is due to the iteration order of searching a mirroring switch from the location being close to the flow monitors.

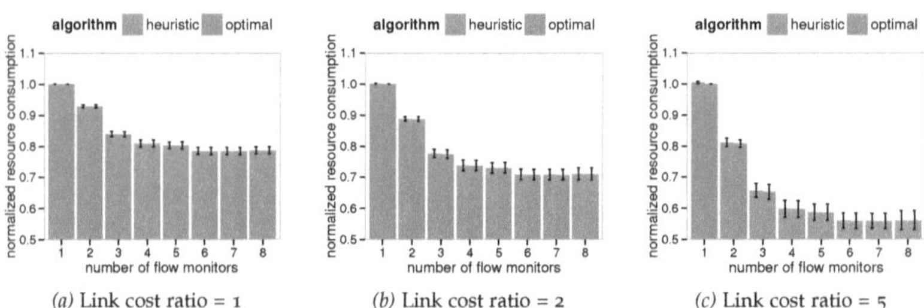

(a) Link cost ratio = 1    (b) Link cost ratio = 2    (c) Link cost ratio = 5

*Figure 3.5:* Impact of the number of flow monitors and the link cost ratio on the resource consumption

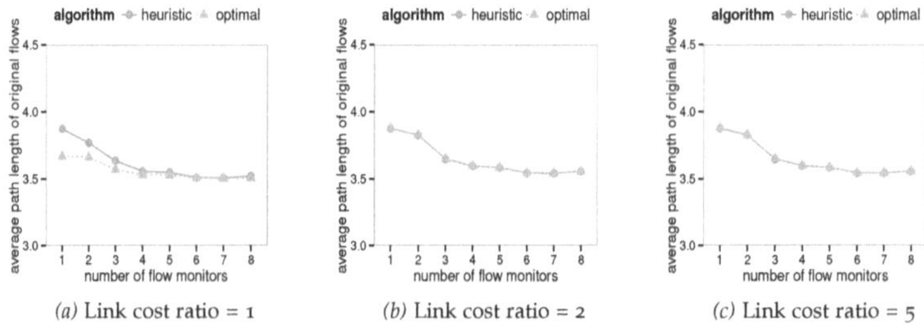

(a) Link cost ratio = 1    (b) Link cost ratio = 2    (c) Link cost ratio = 5

*Figure 3.6:* Impact of the number of flow monitors and the link cost ratio on the path length of original data flows

### 3.4.3.2 *Impact of the number of flow monitors and the link cost ratio*

We vary the number of flow monitors from 1 to 8, and fix the path stretch ratio to 1.5 to allow 50% longer flow paths compared with the shortest ones. We also select the link cost ratio from the discrete value set $\{1, 2, 5\}$.

Figure 3.5 depicts the impact of the number of flow monitors and the link cost ratio on the resource consumption. In each subfigure, we normalize the network resource consumption with the obtained optimal result when there is only one flow monitor. We can see that, regardless of the link cost ratio, increasing the number of flow monitors can always reduce the overall network resource consumption. However, this may bring the issues like increasing the resource consumption on the servers hosting more flow monitors. In this work, the number of flow monitors is a given value for system configuration. It is also possible to integrate the cost of deploying flow monitors into the model, which can be an extension of this work. We observe that the cost of transmission in the monitoring plane is higher, stretching the paths of original data flows helps to reduce a large portion of the overall network resource consumption. We can see that increasing the flow monitor number from 1 to 2 or 3 brings the greatest drop in the resource consumption. After that, adding more flow monitors results in only marginal improvement. Again, we can also see that our heuristic algorithm achieves near optimal results. It only performs slightly worse than the optimal results when only a few flow monitors exist.

Figure 3.6 shows the impact of the number of flow monitors and the link cost ratio on the computed path length of original data flows. In general, we can see that using more flow monitors reduces the paths of original data flows. The reason is that it provides a higher chance that a flow passes through the vicinity of the flow monitors. Compared with the optimal results, our heuristic algorithm computes slightly longer paths of original data flows when the link cost ratio is 1, but achieves almost the same results in the two other scenarios.

### 3.4.3.3 *Baseline strategies comparison*

We compare the following strategies: (1) Optimal FMPSB + Optimal FEMSS (O+O), (2) Optimal FMPSB + Heuristic FEMSS (O+H), (3) Random FMPSB + Optimal FEMSS (R+O), (4) Optimal FMPSB + Random mirroring switch (O+R), (5) Random FMPSB + Random mirroring switch (R+R). In the random flow monitor placement, we randomly choose the locations of flow monitors and bind the switches to them. In the random mirroring switch selection, original data flows follow the shortest paths, but we randomly select the mirroring switches. We configure the link cost ratio to 5 and assume two flow monitors in the network. We chose the path stretch ratio from the set $\{1, 1.5, 2, 3\}$. We show the results of the reduction in the resource consumption achieved with each strategy. The results are normalized by the incurred resource consumption when the system uses the fully random strategy (R+R).

Figure 3.7 depicts the impact of different strategies on the overall resource consumption. The results of the strategies R+R and O+R remain the same for the different path stretch ratios, since the strategy of randomly selecting the mirroring switches does not incorporate this parameter. The strategy R+R leads to the highest network resource consumption, while our consecutive strategies O+O and O+H, achieve the lowest values, even when only the shortest paths are allowed. Only optimizing the placement of the flow monitors or the flow embedding and mirroring switch selection lead to in-between performance. The results also show that increasing the path length stretch ratio can significantly reduce the overall network resource consumption, even when the flow monitor placement is random.

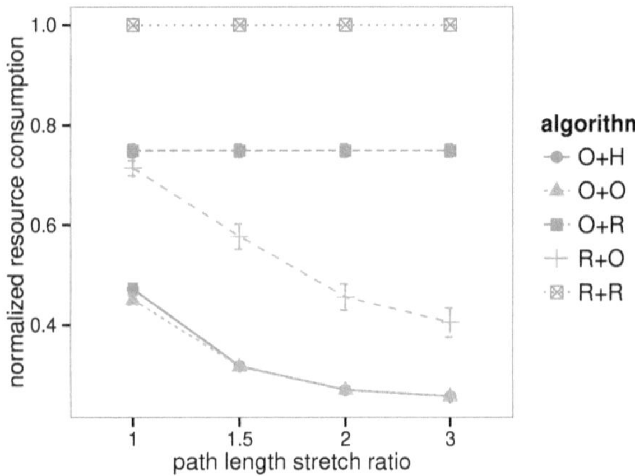


*Figure 3.7:* Performance comparison of difference strategies.

## 3.5 RELATED WORK

In addition to the approaches that optimize the network resource consumption of a monitoring system for SDN in Section 2.3.1, there are several other frameworks that achieve this goal. DISTTM [94] and [209] reduce the number of flow statistic queries and replies by avoiding duplicated measurements on multiple switches for the same flow. OpenNet-Mon [219] polls the edge switches at an adaptive rate to obtain the QoS parameters of flows. Payless [39] also employs an adaptive flow statistics collection mechanism to achieve the balance between the monitoring accuracy and network overhead. As mentioned in the introduction of this chapter, the additional network resources consumed by stretching the paths of original data flows are ignored in these work, which is the focus of this contribution.

## 3.6 CONCLUSION

Mirroring data flows in the network and transmitting the mirrored flows to flow monitors enable in-depth flow packets analysis. However, transmission of original and mirrored data flows consumes network resources. Our main goal is to reduce the overall cost of transmitting both flow types in distinct communication planes. In this chapter, we present REMO, a network monitoring solution that optimizes the global network resource consumption, in the scenario where the original and mirrored data flows are transmitted in separate planes.

We use an ILP model to optimize the flow monitor placement and switch binding so that they reside at central locations in the network. We also use a MILP model to optimize the paths to embed original data flows and the selection of their mirroring switches. In order to overcome the computational complexity of the proposed MILP model, we also design a near-optimal heuristic algorithm for the flow embedding and mirroring switch selection sub-problem. REMO is able to dramatically reduce the global resource consumption, compared with several baseline strategies. Stretching the original data flow paths is particularly useful when it costs more resources to transmit data in the monitoring plane.

It is an interesting direction to integrate the processing and memory limitations of the flow monitors and switches into the model. In addition, exporting flow records, like in IPFIX [43], further reduces the resource consumption but loses the detailed information of the payload data. Depending on the requirement on the granularity of obtained flow information, designing an adaptive network monitoring system is worthy of investigation. The per-packet monitoring system envisioned in this chapter is very similar to the sampling-based approaches, but it mirrors all packets of a flow under monitoring, which is, of course, a simplified assumption. However, the proposed model and algorithm can also apply to sampling-based systems with slight modifications to reduce the overall network resource consumption. For example, if we know the sampling rate, a coefficient (between 0 and 1) can be multiplied to the first expression of Equation 3.5.

CHAPTER 4

---

# REDUCE RESOURCE CONSUMPTION FOR HETEROGENEOUS SDN

---

## 4.1 INTRODUCTION

In Section 2.1.2, we discussed the example scenario in which SDN and hardware component management are jointly used to perform network control, especially for DCNs with flexible topology configuration. SDN has been successully applied to manage networks of computing clusters. Data centers provide computation and storage resources. As we already show in Section 2.1.2, a typical DCN has a layered fat-tree topology with edge switches and core switches that are interconnected via wired high-speed interconnections, such as Infiniband and 10/100BASE-T Ethernet. This topology is however known to lead to performance bottlenecks when large volumes of data need to be transferred (oversubscribed networking) [66].

Two trends recently emerged to improve the performance of DCN. The first, as Figure 2.4a depicts, consists in introducing – typically alongside wired interconnects – wireless connections between switches or servers [88, 90, 114]. This results in *hybrid* (wired/wireless) DCN, which can be reconfigured flexibly at runtime to, e.g., obtain higher throughput. Researchers have already experimented with different technologies, including visible light or 60GHz Radio Frequency (RF) links with beam-steering antennas [90]. A second emerging trend is that of embedding switching functionalities in each server [36, 222]. This *server-centric* architecture makes it no longer necessary to have dedicated switches to forward packets between servers.

The combination of these two innovations leads to what we refer to as *Hybrid, Server-Centric Data Center Networking (HSC-DCN)*. HSC-DCN have the potential to enable highly-adaptive and (thus) energy-efficient computing [70]. The DFG Collaborative Research Center "Highly Adaptive Energy-Efficient Computing (Highly Adaptive Energy-Efficient Computing (HAEC))" investigated an innovative network architecture supporting the emerging category of Micro-Modular Data Centers (MMDCs) enabled by various communication technologies. In the era of edge/fog computing, the computation on the data from IoT devices or autonomous driving is performed at the edge of the network [192]. MMDCs play a critical role in the edge/fog computing [2, 151, 188]. They are deployed at the network edges and usually consist of a just tens or hundreds of servers – only [21]. The presence of wireless links and the flexibility offered by a server-centric architecture imply that the

HSC-DCN can be effectively reconfigured at runtime. This increases the modularity of the data center and leads to lower energy consumption without affecting performance [70].

Although the mentioned related work [88, 91, 228, 254] provide solutions to optimize the transmission performance by alleviating the congestion problem and improving control plane resilience, the resource efficiency problem remains unexplored for such SDN with heterogeneous communication media.

In this chapter, we address the problem of reconfiguring HSC-DCN so that it can route traffic flows between servers in an energy-efficient manner. In conventional data centers, servers and switches – or even individual communication links – can be activated or de-activated on-demand to reduce energy consumption [98]. Thereby, it is necessary to determine how to serve applications' communication demands with as few servers and switches in the active mode as possible. In HSC-DCN, applying this approach requires overcoming an additional challenge. While the mapping between transmitters and receivers is fixed in wired interconnects, wireless transmitters can in general point to a set of different receivers. For instance, when RF links with beam-steering antennas are used, the beams can be steered to point to an arbitrary receiver within a set of feasible ones.

We define the power efficieciency problem existing in HSC-DCN as the *Energy-aware Coflow and Antenna Scheduling* (ECAS) problem. In this chapter, we present its optimal solution – to which we refer to as *ECAS-Opt* – guarantees that the bandwidth demands of the applications generating coflows are met and at the same time as fewer as possible links (and associated hardware components) are activated. The extra flexibility provided by beam-steering antennas allows to create direct flyways between servers so as to reduce the number of activated wired links. We provide proof on the NP-Hardness of the proposed ECAS problem and show that solving this problem is computationally intensive. To overcome such computational complexity, we provide a heuristic version of our algorithm – called *ECAS-Online*. To show the effectiveness of our model and algorithm, we compared with the widely used Directional Routing (DR) algorithm [180] and to a recently proposed Energy-Efficient Greedy Flow assignment Algorithm (EEGFA) [242].

The remainder of this chapter is organized as follows. In Section 4.2, we introduce the necessary background to understand this contribution, including the network topology, power and traffic model, as well as power reduction opportunities in the considered hybrid, micro data center networks. The proposed ECAS problem is solved by using both the optimization and heuristic algorithm in Section 4.3. Evaluation results are presented in Section 4.4.

## 4.2 SYSTEM SETUPS

This section provides the description of the architecture of HSC-DCN and the opportunity of performing resource reduction in this type of SDN. It also gives clear definition of the traffic model and the power model that are used in the formal formulation and heuristic algorithm.

### 4.2.1 *Network topology*

There are many possibilities for the architecture of HSC-DCN. In this chapter, we consider a 3D torus network topology with boards of servers stacked upon each other motivated by the HAEC project [70, 149] and as depicted in Figure 4.1. The address of each server in this topology is given by the three coordinates $(a_x, a_y, a_z)$.

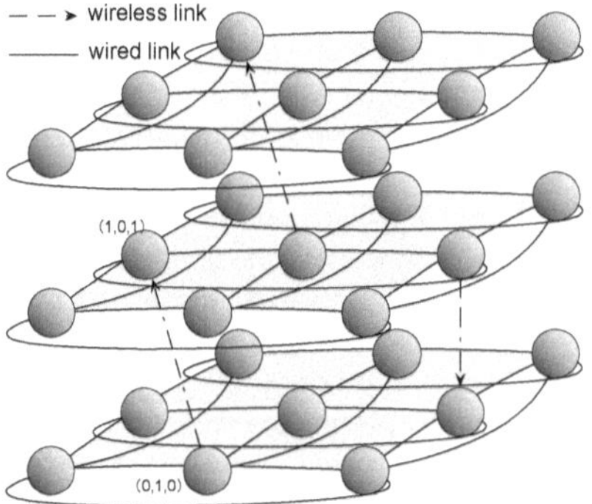


*Figure 4.1:* An exemplary 3x3x3 HSC-DCN topology.

In the exemplary HSC-DCN as shown in Figure 4.1, servers within a board are equipped with a quad-port network interface card and communicate directly through high-speed wired interconnects to their immediate neighbors in the x and y directions. We further assume that servers on adjacent boards can communicate through directional RF links [70, 90, 149]. In this case, each server is equipped with a wireless transceiver featuring a pair of beam-steering antennas for transmitting and receiving. Due to the high operational frequency of the 60GHz RF technology, the path loss of a link is high and penetration capability is limited. Thus, to avoid unstable links caused by obstacles, e.g., other servers or boards, we assume that wireless links can only be established between servers on adjacent boards.

### 4.2.2 *Energy model*

Hardware components used in networking devices in nowadays have the power scaling capacity and low power idle mode. Several scheduling-based network power-efficiency solutions like GreenTE [246] or ElasticTree [98], are built upon the assumption that network hardware elements, such as network cards and its ports, can operate in the active and sleep mode. Similarly, in this chapter, we also assume a server that forwards packets is capable of gradually turning off its Packet Processing Unit (PPU), quad-port network interface card and wireless transceivers. Similar to the *interface-based energy model* defined in [241], we consider the energy consumed by a server to be the sum of three components: (1) a fixed amount of power, $P_s$; (2) the power consumption of wired links, $P_o$; (3) the power consumption of wireless links, $P_w$.

In our model, we follow a practice proposed by other authors in the research area of green data center networks [138, 225, 246]. We approximate the static power consumption of a packet processing unit and its other periphery elements with a fixed, known value, $P_s$. The static power consumption occurs once a server activates its PPU. Shutting down the PPU of a server results in no static energy consumption. According to the measurement results and the power model proposed in [116], the dynamic power consumption of processing a set of flows is linearly proportional to their aggregated flow data rates. Since our model and algorithm take the data rates of a batch of flows as inputs, the total dynamic power consumption always equals to the product of the power consumption per data rate unit and the aggregated rates of all data flows within a batch. As a result, we do not explicitly include the dynamic power consumption incurred by the packet processing workload of the PPUs.

In addition, $P_o$ is proportional to the number of powered-on wired links. It is used to maintain a single port and peripheral circuit for a wired link. The maximum energy consumption spent on wired links is $P_o * n$ for each server, where $n$ stands for the number of connected and activated wired links. In the HSC-DCN shown in Figure 4.1, each server can activate at most four pairs of outgoing and incoming wired links, and $n$ equals to 4.

The value of $P_w$ depends on the on/off status of the wireless transceiver of a server. The power consumption of wireless transceivers can be decomposed into the energy required by the RF front end, analog-to-digital converters, and other components [74]. $P_w$ incurs only if a server establishes a wireless connection and the direction of its associated antenna is appropriately scheduled. Using this energy model, we compute the total energy consumption of a server as:

$$P = P_s * m + P_o * n + P_w * i \tag{4.1}$$

In the formula, $n$ and $i$ are the number of activated wired and wireless links while $m$ encodes the on/off (1/0) status of the server's PPU.

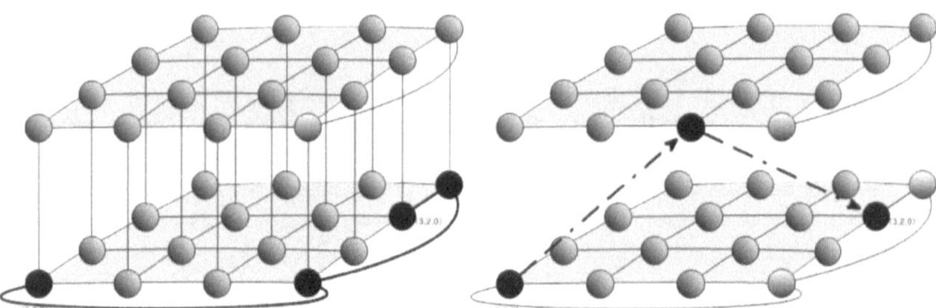

(a) The communication request is routed only through nodes that reside at the same layer.

(b) The communication request is routed through a node that resides at the neighboring layer.

*Figure 4.2:* An example of using link skipping to reduce the number of activated network components and links. It is assumed that there is a communication request from the source $(0,0,0)$ to the destination $(3,2,0)$.

### 4.2.3 *Power reduction opportunities in HSC-DCN*

In this contribution, we focus on and explore the opportunity to reduce the energy consumed during the transmission of data flows in HSC-DCN. Constructing energy-efficient HSC-DCN demands the support of underlying hardware. One effective approach to reduce the energy consumption is to dynamically configure the states (active vs. sleep) of network components, including packet processing engines and peripheral hardware associated with physical network links, during data transmission. The key question is which set of network components should be configured to be in the active state.

In order to reduce the number of activated network components, two energy reduction opportunities exist in HSC-DCN. The first energy reduction opportunity is traffic consolidation. It is a common network traffic engineering approach to use a small number of active network components to serve traffic demands, so as to put the rest of network components into the sleeping mode [225, 246]. This approach is introduced and explained in Section 2.2.3. In our work, we also take the advantage of this basic energy reduction opportunity, and aggregate and route traffic flows through selected active networking components.

The second energy reduction opportunity is *link skipping*, and it is unique in HSC-DCN. The architecture of the 60GHz wireless system has been constantly improved over the past years [123]. The state-of-the-art wireless technology, such as 1 bit sampling [76], makes it possible to achieve ultra-low energy consumption for wireless data transmission. Thus, we assume that the wireless links in HSC-DCN have the similar energy efficiency as the wired links. To fulfill a communication request across the network, instead of activating a chain of the network components belonging to multiple wired links, using direct wireless links as short-cuts can reduce the number of involved wired network components, leading to less energy consumption. Figure 4.2 provides an example of taking advantages of link skipping to reduce the number of activated network components and links. In this example, there exists a communication request from the source $(0,0,0)$ to the destination $(3,2,0)$. Figure 4.2a shows one possible path to route this request by going through only the nodes at the same layer. In this case, 4 nodes and 3 links need to be activated. Figure 4.2b illustrates another path to route this request by using link skipping. One node in another layer is used to relay traffic data from the source to the destination. In this case, 3 nodes and 2 links need to be activated.

### 4.2.4 *Flow model*

The commonly used assumption in energy-efficient networking is that the network controller knows the desired bandwidth demands to transmit data within a period of time [98, 134, 138, 246]. One type of data flows existing in computing clusters is named as *coflows*, which are *"collections of parallel flows"* [36, 38]. Coflows typically occur during intermediate processing stages of specific operations – like parallel joins – when large volumes of data move among servers [36, 38, 174, 252]. Coflows are dominant in data centers that serve big data applications [36, 38, 56]. The coflow information can be obtained through the channel between the network resource provisioner (this concept is introduced in Section 2.2.3) and a big data application manager. The SDN controller accepts information about coflow demands from either a data migration scheduler [174] or a network negotiator [201] as explained in Section 2.2.3. The computed solution to the ECAS problem is distributed to each server node to power on wired links, steer its antenna to establish wireless links and update its forwarding rule table for flows. Once resources for managing coflows are allocated, other traffic flows can also be scheduled using the same routes assigned to coflows or other remaining resources.

### 4.3 OPTIMIZATION MODEL AND ALGORITHM FOR THE ECAS PROBLEM

In this section, we present and describe the optimization model and the heuristic algorithm for solving the ECAS problem.

### 4.3.1 *Formal formulation for the ECAS problem*

The HSC-DCN we consider in this chapter can be represented as a graph $G = (V, E)$, where $V$ represents a set of servers and $E$ is a set of candidate links that can be powered on. $E$ is split in two subsets, $E_o$ and $E_w$. $E_o$ contains all wired links while $E_w$ is the set of all

| Variable | Definition |
| --- | --- |
| $i :< s_i, r_i, d_i >$ | A tuple of a flow request containing source $s_i$, destination $r_i$ and a bandwidth demand $d_i$ and it belongs to a coflow |
| $P_s$ | Static power consumption of the packet processing unit in a server |
| $P_o$ | Power consumption of an active wired link |
| $P_w$ | Power consumption of an active wireless link |
| $E_w$ | A set of wireless links |
| $V$ | A set of servers |
| $E_o$ | A set of wired links |
| $e$ | A link in the set of wired or wireless links |
| $f_e^i$ | $f_e^i = 1$ if the flow $i$ is assigned to the link $e$ |
| $C_e$ | Capacity of wired or wireless links |
| $w_v$ | $w_v = 1$ if the packet processing unit of a server is activated |
| $t_e$ | $t_e = 1$ if a link $e$ is activated |

*Table 4.1:* Variables used in the optimization model and heuristic algorithm of ECAS.

possible wireless links. To differentiate between transmitting and receiving nodes of a link, we represent the extremes of a link as $\text{begin}(e)$ and $\text{end}(e)$. We can then formulate the ECAS problem as the following ILP:

$$\text{minimize} \quad P_s \sum_{v \in V} w_v + P_o \sum_{e \in E_o} t_e + P_w \sum_{e \in E_w} t_e \tag{4.2a}$$

$$\text{subject to} \quad \sum_{e:e \in \text{out}(s_i)} f_e^i = \sum_{e:e \in \text{in}(s_i)} f_e^i + 1 \tag{4.2b}$$

$$\sum_{e:e \in \text{in}(r_i)} f_e^i = \sum_{e:e \in \text{out}(r_i)} f_e^i + 1 \tag{4.2c}$$

$$\sum_{e:e \in \text{out}(v)} f_e^i = \sum_{e:e \in \text{in}(v)} f_e^i = 1, v \notin \{s_i, r_i\} \tag{4.2d}$$

$$\sum_{i} f_e^i d_i \leqslant C_e t_e, e \in E_w \cup E_o \tag{4.2e}$$

$$t_e \leqslant w_{\text{begin}(e)}, t_e \leqslant w_{\text{end}(e)}, e \in E_o \tag{4.2f}$$

$$\sum_{e:e \in \text{out}(v)} t_e \leqslant w_v, \sum_{e:e \in \text{in}(v)} t_e \leqslant w_v, e \in E_w \tag{4.2g}$$

$$f_e^i, t_e, w_v \in \{0, 1\} \tag{4.2h}$$

Table 4.1 summarizes the definition of all variables used in the problem formulation. Thereby, Equation (4.2a) is the objective function and represents the goal to minimize overall energy consumption of HSC-DCN. The input to this ILP formulation is a batch of flow requests belonging to a single coflow. A flow request $i$ is expressed as a tuple containing source address $s_i$, destination address $r_i$ and bandwidth demand $d_i$. The total number of flow requests within a coflow is referred to as the *width* of the coflow [252]. The solution of the ECAS problem is a set of paths, each indicated by $f_e^i$ for the corresponding flow request $i$.

The solution also generates a schedule to power up the PPU of a server and links, indicated by $w_v$ and $t_e$. Constraint (4.2b, 4.2c) and Constraint (4.2d) are constraints that make only one path to be selected for each flow. The calculated paths must be pruned to get the simple path that does not contain loops. Constraint (4.2e) guarantees that the aggregated bandwidth demand on a single link does not exceed its capacity. Constraint (4.2f) and Constraint (4.2g) ensure that the PPU of a server will not be completely powered off if one of its associated links is in the on status.

We assume that both transmitting and receiving antennas belonging to a wireless link operate in a directional way. Han *et al.* [91] point out that a mmWave link can be configured to run at relatively low speed in comparison of their actual channel capacity, the resulting connection is so reliable that it can be treated as if it were a wired one. In order to obtain highly reliable mmWave links, both transmitter and receiver need to perform beam-locking to achieve high antenna gain on both ends of a wireless link [79]. Thus, the schedule for antennas' directions should guarantee one-to-one mapping for transmitting and receiving antennas, as also done in [114]. Accordingly, Constraint (4.2g) guarantees that the transmitting and receiving antennas participate in at most one wireless link each.

### 4.3.2 *NP Hardness of the ECAS problem*

To prove that the ECAS problem is NP-Hard, we show that the results of the ECAS problem can be obtained by repeatedly solving a basic NP-Hard problem with different inputs. In the ECAS formulation, the physical topology of the network is unknown beforehand because of the need to schedule the directions of antennas and fulfill Constraint 5.1g. To overcome this topology uncertainty, we can precompute a valid wireless link set, $E'_w$, containing no conflicting wireless links, and use $E'_w$ as a part of physical topology input for the following refined ECAS-Sub problem. We denote $E_w^+$ to represent all possible wireless link sets, thus $E'_w$ belongs to $E_w^+$.

---

**Algorithm 3** ECAS-Sub algorithm

---

1: **for** $E'_w$ in $E^+_w$ **do**
2:     Solve the ECAS-Sub problem using the wireless link set $E'_w$ as a part of physical topology input
3: **end for**
4: Choose the ECAS solution, that leads to the minimal power consumption, from results computed in the above iterations

---

$$\text{minimize} \quad P_s \sum_{v \in V} w_v + P_o \sum_{e \in E_o} t_e + P_w \sum_{e \in E'_w} t_e \tag{4.3a}$$

$$\text{subject to} \quad \sum_{e:e \in out(s_i)} f^i_e = \sum_{e:e \in in(s_i)} f^i_e + 1 \tag{4.3b}$$

$$\sum_{e:e \in in(r_i)} f^i_e = \sum_{e:e \in out(r_i)} f^i_e + 1 \tag{4.3c}$$

$$\sum_{e:e \in out(v)} f^i_e = \sum_{e:e \in in(v)} f^i_e = 1, v \notin \{s_i, r_i\} \tag{4.3d}$$

$$\sum_i f^i_e d_i \leqslant C_e t_e, e \in E'_w \cup E_o \tag{4.3e}$$

$$t_e \leqslant w_{begin(e)}, t_e \leqslant w_{end(e)}, e \in E_o \cup E'_w \tag{4.3f}$$

$$f^i_e, t_e, w_v \in \{0, 1\} \tag{4.3g}$$

The adaptation from the ECAS problem to the ECAS-Sub problem is that we remove Constraint (4.2g), which leads to using precomputed non-conflicting wireless links in the model, instead of using the set containing all possible wireless links. Obtaining the final optimal results requires to repeatedly solve this ECAS-Sub problem by iterating through each precomputed $E'_w$, as shown in Algorithm 3. The ECAS-Sub problem in Algorithm 3 is actually a Minimum Edges Routing (MER) problem, which has been proved to be NP-Hard [78]. Since solving the ECAS problem is equivalent to solving a serial of NP-Hard MER problems, we can conclude that the ECAS problem is also NP-Hard.

### 4.3.3 *Heuristic algorithm for the ECAS problem*

Due to its NP-Hardness, solving the formulated ECAS problem by directly using an optimizer requires a considerable amount of time. Traffic flows would thus experience huge delays (ranging from minutes to hours) if they had to wait for a solution to be computed. To cope with this problem, we develop a heuristic algorithm, named ECAS-Online, that provides an approximate solution of the formulated ILP and drastically reduces computation time. The algorithm is still developed to deal with batches of flow requests since we perform scheduling for the coflows and currently we do not consider the sequentially arrived flow requests. We use the term, *online algorithm*, to indicate the fact that its execution time is very short compared with our optimal solution, thus it is suitable to deploy for an online network management system.

The principle of searching an energy-efficient scheduling solution with ECAS-Online is to use already powered-on packet processing units of servers and links to serve coflow demands as much as possible without dramatically decreasing network performance. The authors of [242] proposed a greedy flow assignment algorithm to achieve power-efficiency for DCNs with the fat-tree topology equipped with only wired links. This algorithm greedily assigns flows to communication links to obtain locally minimal energy consumption. However, our experiments show that this greedy algorithm generates excessive long paths for flows, which causes additional processing delays along the path due to packet switching performed on more intermediate servers. In order to achieve the balance between the energy consumption and network performance, particularly the length of paths experienced by flows, we construct a heuristic algorithm, named ECAS-Online, based on the $A^*$ algorithm [95, 173].

The $A^*$ algorithm is a path planning algorithm for mobile robotics [49], which falls into the category of best-first greedy algorithms. This algorithm combines heuristic searching and shortest path searching, and each candidate step is evaluated with the function:

$$f(v) = h(v) + g(v) \tag{4.4}$$

$h(v)$ is the distance, e.g., Manhatten or Euclidean distance, of the currently evaluated step to the final destination. $g(v)$ stands for the length of the path from the originated point to the currently evaluated step through the chosen step sequence [63]. The step with the lowest value of $f(v)$ is selected as the next step to move. The distances used in this algorithm can be modified to represent other metrics. Since we consider both potentially increased energy consumption incurred by choosing a node and its distance to the flow destination, the $A^*$ algorithm is selected to concatenate both metrics.

ECAS-Online activates communication links and finds paths for single flows one after another, when it processes communication requests of a coflow. ECAS-Online uses a score value to determine if selecting a neighbouring server and corresponding candidate link would improve the overall power consumption efficiency as well as bring flows closer to their destination. More specifically, we define a weighted score function:

$$g(f, n) = k * e^{E(n)/E_{max}} + (1 - k)e^{d(n)/d_f} \tag{4.5}$$

In this function, $g(f, n)$ stands for the score of the server $n$ during the scheduling for the flow $f$. $E(n)$ is the overall power consumption if the server $n$ is selected as the next

---

**Algorithm 4** ECAS-Online algorithm

---

**Input:** a batch of communication requests $F$ containing $f_i :< s_i, r_i, d_i >$, a set of all wired and possible wireless links $M_{all}$.

**Output:** a set $M_{power\_on}$ containing powered on links, a link assignment plan $R_i$ for a flow $f_i$.

**Initialize:**

1: $F(0), F(1)...F(n) = \phi$    //Groups of $f_i$ based on their distance along Z axis between $s_i$ and $d_i$

2: $M_{power\_on} = \phi$

**Main procedure:**

3: **for** $f_i$ in $F$ **do**

4:    $d_z^i = \|a_z^{r_i} - a_z^{s_i}\|$    //Compute distance along Z axis between $s_i$ and $d_i$

5:    Insert $f_i$ into $F(n)$ if $d_z^i$ equals to $n$

6: **end for**

7: **for** $f_i$ in $F(n), F(n-1)...F(0)$ **do**

8:    $E(s_i) = cost(s_i)$, $d(s_i) = d_f$

9:    Compute $g[f_i, s_i]$ based on $E(s_i)$ and $d(s_i)$

10:    **for all** $v$ in $V - \{s_i\}$ **do**

11:       $g[f_i, v] = MAX\_VALUE$

12:    **end for**

13:    $S = \phi$, $Q = V$

14:    **while** $Q$ is not empty **do**

15:       $u = minScore(Q)$

16:       $S = S \cup \{u\}$, $Q = Q - \{u\}$

17:       **if** $u$ equals to $r_i$ **then**

18:          **break**

19:       **end if**

20:       $M_{power\_on} = M_{power\_on} \cup \{e(pre, u)\}$

21:       $capacity[e(pre, u)] = capacity[e(pre, u)] - d_i$

22:       **if** $e(pre, u)$ is a wireless link **then**

23:          $M_{all} = M_{all} - \{e_{RF}(pre,)\} - \{e_{RF}(,u)\}$

24:       **end if**

25:       $prev = u$

26:       **for** $e(u, v)$ in $M_{all}$ **do**

27:          **if** $e(u, v)$ exists in $M_{power\_on}$ **then**

28:             $E(v) = E[u]$

29:          **else if** $v$ is powered on **then**

30:             $E(v) = E[u] + cost(u, v)$

31:          **else**

32:             $E(v) = E[u] + cost(u, v) + cost(v)$

33:          **end if**

| | |
|---|---|
| 34: | Compute $g[f_i, v]$ based on $E(v)$ and $d(v)$ |
| 35: | **if** $capacity[e(u, v)] < d_i$ **then** |
| 36: | $g[f_i, v] = MAX\_VALUE$ |
| 37: | **end if** |
| 38: | **end for** |
| 39: | **end while** |
| 40: | $R_i = S$ |
| 41: | **end for** |
| 42: | **return** $E_{power\_on}$, all $R_i$ |

forwarding hop, depending on the status of both the PPU of this server and its associated link. $E_{max}$ is the power consumption when all PPUs and links of servers are powered on. $d(n)$ is the euclidean distance between the candidate server $n$ and flow destination. $d_f$ is the euclidean distance between the flow source and destination. We use parameter $k$ belonging to the range $(0, 1]$ to tune the balance between the importance of the network energy consumption and flow path length.

Wireless links between boards tend to be used as energy-efficient shortcuts for flows originating and terminating on the hosts of the same board. In this case, there may not exist enough bandwidth to be allocated for flows that need to traverse across boards along the $z$ direction. Thus, our algorithm gives priority to flows that originate and terminate on servers of different boards and constructs powered-on paths for them first. In order to do so, the communication requests of single flows are classified and sorted based on the distance along the $z$ direction between their source and destination (lines 3-6).

Lines 7-42 activate and select wired and wireless links to forward each flow based on the computed score of each server. Lines 26-33 describe the rules to compute the estimated overall power consumption of neighbouring vertices. If a link with a neighbouring vertex has been powered on, we consider that using this link does not incur additional power consumption, otherwise we need to activate this powered-off link and add additional $cost(u, v)$ (lines 27-30). Depending on the on/off status of the PPU of the server at the end of a link, additional basic power consumption, $cost(v)$ is included (line 32). The scores of neighbouring vertices are computed based on its estimated power consumption and its distance from the flow destination (line 34). Additionally, ECAS-Online also keeps track of remaining bandwidth of each link (line 22) and only selects a link that can meet the bandwidth requirement of a flow (lines 35-36).

In order to guarantee one-to-one mapping for transmitting and receiving antennas, ECAS-Online maintains a set $M_{all}$ containing all possible links as candidates, even those wireless links sharing end points. If one wireless link is chosen to be powered on and the directions of its corresponding antennas are configured, we remove other possible wireless links involving either ends of this selected wireless link from $M_{all}$ (line 22-24).

The complexity of ECAS-Online is $O(|V||L||F|)$, where $|V|$ is the total number of servers in HSC-DCN, $|L|$ is the number of all possibly connected links with a server and $|F|$ is the total number of concurrently transmitted flows.

## 4.4 EVALUATION

In this section, we report the evaluation of the proposed model and algorithm for the ECAS problem using simulations. We first describe the simulation setup and then report our results.

### 4.4.1 Implementation and settings

The proposed network topology, model and algorithm for the ECAS problem are implemented in OMNeT++ [168] and we use Gurobi [84] as the optimizer for ILP. As a proof of concept and due to the fact that a MMDCN consists of hundred of servers, we choose two topologies, 4x4x3 and 6x6x3, of HSC-DCN as shown in Figure 4.1 for the simulations. These two topologies allow us to observe the performance of our model and algorithm on different-sized HSC-DCN. They also allow to complete the simulations within reasonable time, especially when to compute the baseline optimal scheduling results. The large amount of time to compute the optimal solution is because that, in the novel architecture we consider, there are much more additional possible flyway links formed by 60GHz links and thus a larger number of candidate paths that can be taken by a data flow. By performing these evaluations, we show that the designed heuristic algorithm is suitable to deal with such complexity existing in a highly adaptive and resource-efficient HSC-DCN.

The implemented HSC-DCN simulation framework allows configuration of the arbitrary size along three dimensions for HSC-DCN. The token bucket based algorithm [178] is implemented for flow bandwidth reservation. Similar to the assumptions used in [88] and [91], we assume that both wired and directional wireless links can achieve the transmission rate of 10 Gbps and the bit error rate as 0. A dynamic transmission rate based on the channel quality, such as signal-to-interference-plus-noise ratio (SINR) can be further integrated into the model. The simulation adopts the many-to-many communication pattern for a single coflow [252]. We also use random flows, similar to [91], in which the size of each flow is fixed as 50 MB but the source and destination of each flow are randomly selected. In order to estimate the bandwidth requirement for flows, a soft deadline to complete the transmission of coflows is used and configured as 1 second. The width of a coflow, which is the number of concurrent transmitted flows, varies from 10 to 50 for both topologies. In order to avoid biased results caused by randomly generated flow pattern, we repeat simulations on each scheduling algorithm for 3 rounds by configuring different seeds for the random number generator.

*Table 4.2:* Computation time of scheduling algorithms for different coflow width in the 4x4x3 topology

|  | Width of Coflows | | | | |
|---|---|---|---|---|---|
|  | 10 | 20 | 30 | 40 | 50 |
| DR | 0.07ms | 0.11ms | 0.14ms | 0.21ms | 0.24ms |
| EEGFA | 5.47ms | 9.35ms | 13.1ms | 15.0ms | 19.3ms |
| ECAS-Online | 1.86ms | 2.73ms | 3.34ms | 4.15ms | 4.43ms |
| ECAS-Opt | 7.44s | 2.79min | 11.1min | 0.43h | 1.62h |

In the evaluation, we compare the simulation results of our ECAS-Opt and ECAS-Online with one widely used 3D torus network routing algorithm, DR, and EEGFA proposed in [242]. We experiment with different values of the parameter k in the score function and we configure it as 0.9 to maximize the performance of the ECAS-Online algorithm. In order to perform DR algorithm, wireless links are vertically formed between direct neighbours locating on different layers in a static way. Flows are firstly forwarded along the z direction to reach the same boards of their destination server, then flows are forwarded along the x and y direction until they arrive at their destinations. The EEGFA algorithm greedily looks for the most energy-efficient paths in local scopes for flows. In the rest part of this section, we report evaluation results on the computation time of the algorithms, energy consumption, the path length generated by the algorithms and coflow completion time.

### 4.4.2 *Computation time*

Table 4.2 shows the average computation time of the scheduling algorithms when we change coflow width in the scenario. We show the result for the 4x4x3 topology. The computation time of scheduling algorithms increases as more concurrent flows need to be transmitted. As expected, ECAS-Opt requires huge amount of time to obtain the optimal results. It takes seconds to hours to obtain the optimal results for the 4x4x3 topology, even days for the 6x6x3 topology. DR is able to generate scheduling results within 1ms due to its simplicity. ECAS-Online is slower than DR but faster than EEGFA for different coflow width. This fact suggests that ECAS-Online is suitable to be implemented in the real system without incurring large delays, because that the arriving batches of communication requests can be processed in a timely manner. The constraint on scheduling delays depends on the application transmitting data. For example, if the application has a low tolerance on the scheduling delay, the controller should even choose the DR algorithm without considering power efficiency.

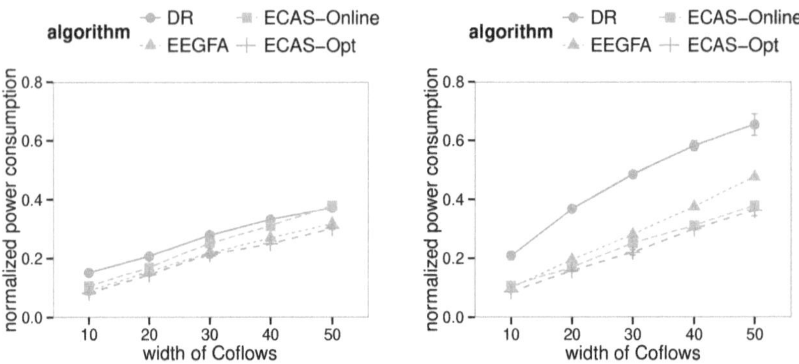

(a) Normalized power consumption of 4x4x3 HSC-DCN.    (b) Normalized power consumption of 6x6x3 HSC-DCN.

*Figure 4.3*: Normalized energy consumption produced by scheduling algorithms in 4x4x3 and 6x6x3 topologies.

### 4.4.3 *Power consumption*

Power consumption of HSC-DCN is computed by summing up basic power consumed by all powered-on PPUs of servers and power used to maintain active wired and wireless links. For the convenience of comparison, the power consumption produced by scheduling algorithms is normalized by the total power consumed by the network of a fully powered-on HSC-DCN. Figure 4.3 depicts the average value and standard deviation of normalized power consumption during three rounds of simulations, for both topologies. In general, this figure shows that the network consumes more power as the width of a coflow increases, since more processing units of servers and links need to become active to serve increasing number of concurrent flows. ECAS-Opt achieves the lowest network power consumption while DR generates scheduling results that lead to higher energy consumption compared with other algorithms. ECAS-Online is able to generate scheduling plans leading to less network power consumption than DR but performs slightly worse than EEGFA since it tries to achieve balance between power consumption and path length for flows. In addition, we can observe that the normalized power consumption results generated by different algorithms converge quickly in the 4x4x3 HSC-DCN. The reason is that, in the 4x4x3 HSC-DCN, the percentage of activated PPUs and links increases faster when more flows enter the network. On the contrary, to fulfill the communication requests of the same width of coflows, there is still a large portion of inactivated PPUs and links in the 6x6x3 HSC-DCN.

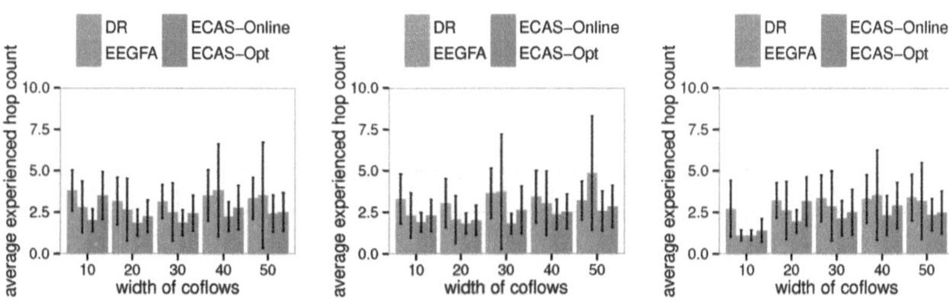

*(a)* Hop count statistics for the round #1, 2 and 3 in 4x4x3 HSC-DCN.

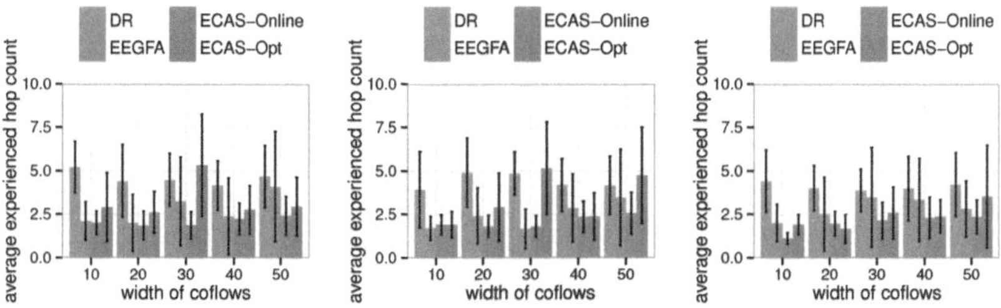

*(b)* Hop count statistics for the round #1, 2 and 3 in 6x6x3 HSC-DCN.

*Figure 4.4:* Hop count statistics for the flows in 4x4x3 and 6x6x3 topologies

### 4.4.4 Path length

The length of used paths to forward flows affects coflow completion time. Flows forwarded along longer paths experience larger completion time for transmission due to additional processing time on intermediate servers. Figure 4.4 shows the impact of the scheduling algorithms on the path length experienced by coflows in each round. The difference of hop counts in each round is caused by diversely generated traffic patterns. Figure 4.4 shows that ECAS-Online is able to select relatively short paths for flows in each round, compared with other algorithms. The reason is that ECAS-Online integrates the distance between the next hop server and destination server into the score function, thus it is able to establish short-cut paths using wireless links. DR and EEGFA generate relatively longer paths for coflows. ECAS-Opt attempts to minimize the energy consumption by reusing already powered-on links as much as possible even if those links bring flows away from their destination. Besides that, in general, the average path length experienced by the flows

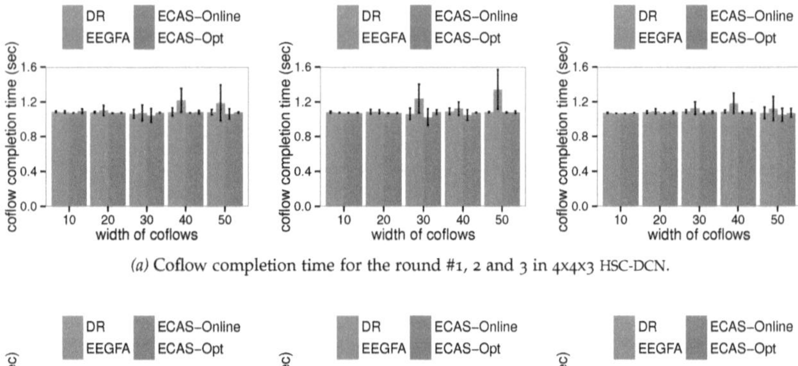

(a) Coflow completion time for the round #1, 2 and 3 in 4x4x3 HSC-DCN.

(b) Coflow completion time for the round #1, 2 and 3 in 6x6x3 HSC-DCN.

Figure 4.5: Coflow completion time in 4x4x3 and 6x6x3 topologies.

in the 6x6x3 HSC-DCN is greater than that in the 4x4x3 HSC-DCN, which is due to the its relatively larger network size.

### 4.4.5 Coflow completion time

Coflow Completion Time (CCT) is defined as the average value of transferring time of all flows within a coflow [252]. We use this metric to show the overhead and impact brought by our current system design and implementation on the network performance. Figure 4.5 shows that CCTs of all coflows are larger than the soft completion deadline, 1s. It is caused by the overhead (e.g., headers, signaling) of the network protocol, especially Transmission Control Protocol (TCP), in the implementation, as well as accumulated processing delays on each forwarding server. In this figure, ECAS-Online is able to achieve the lowest CCTs, which confirms the results that it generates relatively shorter paths for coflows and did not bring congestions on each link. However, we can also observe some abnormal spikes of

CCT, such as the result of EEGFA when the width of the coflow is 50 in the second round. We investigate this phenomenon and find that it is due to the congestion of the packet buffer in the PPU. When the packet buffer congestion happens, some flow packets get dropped, leading to the degradation of the TCP bandwidth.

## 4.5 RELATED WORK

In this section, we provide background and related work on the architecture of HSC-DCN, approaches and challenges to save energy in HSC-DCN.

### 4.5.1 *Hybrid server-centric data center networks*

A server-centric data center network architecture allows dense deployment of servers, thus it is suitable for designing a compact yet powerful computing cluster. The topology of 3D torus is a widely used High Performance Computing (HPC) interconnection. It is introduced by CamCube [45] and NovaCube [226] to build a general-purpose data center. Compared with conventional tree-based DCN, a server-centric DCN is more resilient to link and server failures thanks to the existence of redundant paths among servers and absence of critical network devices such as core switches. In addition, studies show that a server-centric DCN can support on-path aggregation to reduce network traffic for data analysis applications like MapReduce [46, 222].

The millimetre wave (mmWave) wireless communication technology provides large bandwidth over short ranges. It operates in unlicensed spectrum bands, making it feasible to integrate into existing DCN on the market [90]. The mmWave RF technology uses narrow beams, thus it can significantly reduce interference among antennas even in the close proximities of servers. Additionally, narrow beams can be steered mechanically by rotating parts of antenna circuits or electrically by using scanned array [44] to create on-demand links among networking devices in DCN [114]. Integrating beam-steering mmWave wireless links into the architecture design helps to further improve the flexibility and modularity of a server-centric data center to make it possible to build a data center using 'boxes' [70, 149] or 'containers' [239]. These flexible wireless links provide additional network resource and serve as 'shortcuts' to alleviate the hotspot problem, depending on traffic load in DCN [88]. Firefly [89] is a solution that manages the wireless connections in DCN to satisfy communication demands in the network. It relies on SDN controller to first obtain demand information, then jointly perform topology selection by determining transceiver-receiver pairs and traffic engineering to route the volumes of traffic. Rush [91] is a centralized SDN solution that jointly routes flows and schedules wireless directional antenna to achieve low congestion levels in hybrid DCN. Again, RUSH performs cross-layer network control by planning flow paths, scheduling the orientations of the radio and assigning proper working time for them. Compared with Firefly and RUSH that use heterogeneous transmission medium to transfer application data, the authors of [228, 254] propose to use the wireless part of hybrid DCN as the *control plane* to transmit control flows of SDN. They both developed centralized algorithms to instruct directional wireless links to form a connected graph and compute routing paths for control flows.

### 4.5.2 *Energy saving for HSC-DCN*

Several authors proposed the approach to reduce energy consumption of DCN by turning off or putting temporarily unused network devices and communication links into the sleeping mode [98, 134, 138, 246]. In [138], the authors integrate reliability constraints into the model of energy optimization and solve it by gradually shutting down unused links after the reliability of selected paths is achieved. The length of paths assigned to flows is not considered and the solution generated for HSC-DCN could lead to larger end-to-end delay and slower transferring of coflows. Wang *et al.* [225] propose algorithms relying on the structural properties of the fat-tree topology, thus it is not suitable for server-centric DCN. The work in [246] is most similar to our consideration and it tries to achieve the balance between the energy consumption and path length. In oder to reduce the computational complexity of the model, the authors restrict the searching space of flow paths as the k shortest ones. Solving the optimization problem with the reduced size, however, still costs considerable time in the scale from several seconds to minutes. These existing energy-aware optimization algorithms also face unique challenges in HSC-DCN. First of all, there are more candidate links and paths available in HSC-DCN due to the large amount of possible directions to steer beams. This fact makes the searching space of formulated problem larger compared with conventional DCN built with physically fixed wired links. In addition, candidate RF links counter the occupation problem, in which one directional antenna cannot involve in multiple established RF links at the same time due to the necessity of beam locking, as pointed out by [79, 88, 114] and [91]. Our model and algorithm share similarities with existing approaches but take these unique challenges into consideration.

## 4.6 CONCLUSION

We investigate the problem of energy-aware coflow and antenna scheduling in a hybrid (wired/wireless) server-centric data center network. We formulate this problem as an integer linear program based on a composite energy model. The goal is to minimize energy consumption by powering on as few packet processing units of servers and links as possible. We consider bandwidth constraints on links and the occupation problem when using directional antennas. We further propose an heuristic algorithm to reduce the computational complexity of our optimal solution. Our simulation results show that, with respect to representative competitors, our approach achieves lower energy consumption and generates shorter paths – and thus lower completion time – for coflows. It is a promising direction to consider heavier traffic loads as well as handling the co-existence of multiple coflows.

CHAPTER 5

---

# RESOURCE OPTIMIZATION USING SELF-ADAPTIVE ALGORITHMS

---

## 5.1 INTRODUCTION

As we already discussed and presented in Section 2.3.2.1 and Section 4, combining flexible traffic engineering and dynamic adaptation of operation status of devices is able to reduce power consumption of a network. The commonly used approaches to reduce network power consumption are designing energy-efficient routing mechanisms and adapting the operation modes of network devices, including packet processing units, line cards, transmitters of links and their peripheral circuits, to the sleep mode or low-power mode.

Network management frameworks, such as GreenTE [246], ElasticTree [98], EEGFA [242] and FGH [71], relies on the optimization models or heuristic algorithms to compute power-efficient solutions. However, directly solving the optimization model for each batch of communication demands costs seconds even hours as we show in Chapter 4. Some heuristic algorithms take advantages of the properties of a network topology, thus they are not applicable for networks with a different topology [138]. In addition, due to the strict constraints defined in the optimization model and heuristic algorithm, not every possible combination of traffic demands can be solved, which leads to the failure of computation.

Machine learning, particularly deep learning, has achieved great popularity and success in many fields such as computer vision [221], natural language processing [244] and robotics [206]. Recently, one of the branches of deep learning, Deep Reinforcement Learning (DRL), attracts attentions of the network research community. Unlike traffic engineering frameworks leveraging supervised learning [146, 255], DRL-based network optimization approaches do not need a dataset containing historical operation data, e.g., routing decisions taken by deterministic algorithms. Ideally, without much prior knowledge of a network and its environment, these self-adaptive intelligent frameworks are able to gradually learn a network management policy that handles network dynamics, such as constantly varying network workload, by the method of trial-and-error. In this context, the work presented in this chapter attempts to answer the question: *is the state-of-the-art deep reinforcement learning technique suitable for improving networking power efficiency that is achieved by the commonly used approach of flow consolidation?*

Existing DRL-based traffic engineering and network management frameworks, such as DeepConf [187] and those presented in [203, 235], focus on reducing packet delays. These approaches for optimizing the performance of networks via traffic engineering are built upon Deep Deterministic Policy Gradients (DDPG) [137] and Asynchronous Advantage Actor-Critic (A3C) [155], which are designed for a single agent. More specifically, the controller uses one learning agent to take multiple actions at the same time for the whole network (assigning link weights) [203, 235]. Afterwards, the routing paths are searched based on the calculated link weights.

In this chapter, we propose that, from the perspective of each flow, data flows need to *cooperate* or *compete* by selecting their corresponding paths to achieve traffic engineering goals, which can be referred as a Multi-Agent System (MAS). Each data flow can be modelled as an agent that selects its path from a set of precomputed shortest paths, which leads to a reduced search space for solutions. As a result, we firstly investigate the above described problem and present a DRL-based power optimization framework named *DeepGreen*. In the current design, DeepGreen performs joint scheduling of routing paths and operation status of network devices so as to reduce the power resource consumption in a data center network. Since we model the network and a group of data flows as a MAS, we select a DRL algorithm named Branching Dueling Q-Networks (BDQ) [211] as the fundation of the core modeling algorithm, due to its capability to control multiple agents interacting with each other.

Our evaluation results show that, achieving power efficiency in a standard DCN architecture via flow consolidation while maintaining low end-to-end delays is a difficult task for the deep reinforcement learning approaches considered in this chapter. We find that they are outperformed by the classical optimal and heuristic algorithms. The multi-agent modeling approach in DeepGreen is able, to some extent, to provide solutions that lead to power reduction and maintain low end-to-end delays. However, it cannot always generate the most power-efficient solutions when facing very dynamic traffic volumes and hence its average performance is not as competitive as that of the classical algorithms.

The remainder of the chapter is structured as follows: Section 5.2 describes the network setups and basic idea to conserve power consumption via flow consolidation. Section 5.3 provides the formal model and Section 5.4 provides the description of DRL-based formulation. We provide evaluation results and detailed discussion in Section 5.5. Finally, we summarize related work in Section 5.6 and conclude this chapter in Section 5.7.

## 5.2 SCENARIO AND ASSUMPTIONS

In this section, we describe the network setups and the basic idea to reduce power consumption in a fat-tree based software-defined data center network.

### 5.2.1 *Network setups*

In constrast to the hybrid network architecture investigated in Chapter 4, this chapter considers a SDN-based data center network of the classical fat-tree topology, as shown in Figure 5.1. We already briefly inroduced the fat-tree topology in Section 2.1.2.2. In this network architecture, a network consists of three layers of switches, namely edge switches, aggregation switches and core switches. Edge switches usually directly connect with servers, and hence are called Top-of-Rack switches that reside at the leaf location of the network. Aggregation switches are responsible of aggregating traffic flows from the edge switches within the same pod. Core switches are located at the most upper layer of the network architecture and exchange data among pods. The configuration of the number of each types of switches is not random but follow a set of rules. A $K - ary$ fat-tree indicates that K pods exist in the network, and each pod consists of $K/2$ edge switches and $K/2$ aggregation switches. The total number of core switches is $(K/2)^2$. The switches are connected by Ethernet or Infiniband. The advantage of the fat-tree DCN is that it can provide uniform network capacity with low-cost devices due to using of relatively low-speed switches at the edge and aggregation levels. Meanwhile, it also provides great scalability to increase the size of the network, as well as free selection of multiple paths for data packets [66].

### 5.2.2 *Basic idea to reduce power consumption*

One opportunity, which is identified by many research articles, to reduce power consumption of a richly connected DCN is energy-aware routing. In this approach, a network management system built upon SDN to perform cross-layer coordination of power states of networking devices and routing paths of data flows. This basic idea of conserving power consumption in DCN is motivated by two observed facts. The first observation is that power consumption of network devices remain relatively static despite that their traffic workloads vary over time [98]. The second observation is that many modern networking devices support dynamic power management at the silicon level, such as clock scaling and voltage scaling, and device power management can be be integrated into standard SDN protocols [253].

These two facts indicate that it is possible to reduce the overall power consumption by putting some components in networking devices into the sleeping mode when there is low even no traffic workload. Similar to existing research articles [98, 134], the basic idea behind this chapter to reduce power consumption for a SDN-based DCN is aggregating data flows to go through a set of selected network components in the wake-up mode so as to make the rest devices of a network work in the sleeping mode, as illustrated in Chapter 2.3.2.1. This approach contradicts another important network optimization goal, congestion mitigation,

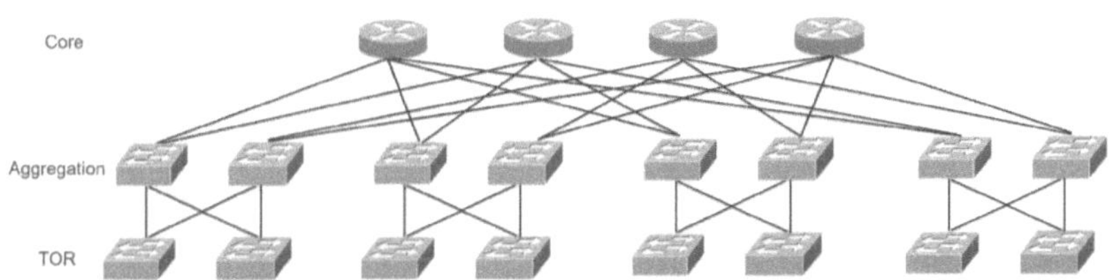


*Figure 5.1:* SDN network that has the typical fat-tree topology that only consists of Ethernet connections

which is usually achieved by balancing data transmission workloads among network links and nodes. As a result, reducing power consumption of DCN should not cause a significant increase in network congestion.

## 5.3 FORMAL MODEL

This section provides a description of power and traffic models that are used throughout this chapter. It also provides a formal model that optimally solves the power efficiency problem in software-defined data center networks. The models introduced in this chapter are similar to those presented in Chapter 4 but do not include the constraints caused by introducing wireless links into the network architecture.

### 5.3.1 *Power model and traffic model*

A generic yet widely used power model for a network switch in DCN categorizes the power consumption into the static and dynamic parts [241]. Depending on which components of a switch are configured in the sleeping mode, the static part refers to the power consumption of the line-card and periphery fabric, and the dynamic part refers to the power consumption of device ports and interfaces that directly connect with another networking device. In order to reduce power consumption of a switch, both ports at the end of a link are deactivated when there is no inbound and outbound traffic on this link. Furthermore, when all associated ports of a device enter the sleeping mode, the same device's line-card and periphery fabric can be also configured in the sleeping mode to further reduce the power consumption. We use $P_s$ to represent the static part and $P_d$ to represent the dynamic part of power consumption. As a result, the total amount of power consumption of a switch is calculated as: $P = n * P_s + m * P_d$, where $n$ is a binary value indicating if the line-card and its periphery fabric are activated or not, and $m$ is the number of ports that are activated.

A SDN controller obtains the information about traffic in the network either by performing real-time monitoring on current workloads or explicitly accepting bandwidth demands from a network resource provisioner, as discussed in section 2.2.3. In this work, a controller of DCN receives a traffic matrix consisting of bandwidth demands among ToR switches. These demand requests arrive in the batch mode. A demand request, $i :< s_i, r_i, d_i >$ indicates the volume of requested bandwidth, the source ToR switch and destination ToR switch. Delimitrou *et al.* [57] analyzed the network workload traces in Microsoft's data centers and use the hierarchical spatial Markov chain model to describe the traffic properties among racks and servers. In this work, the controller performs traffic engineering and schedules the routing paths at the granularity of data flows among ToR switches. Hence, we model the bandwidth demand between each pair of ToR with a Markov chain for the synthetic generation of data packets.

### 5.3.2  *Problem formulation*

In this chapter, the goal to perform traffic engineering and network configuration is to reduce the overall network power consumption when facing dynamic communication demands among servers of DCN. However, one of the consequences of aggregating traffic flows into a selected set of devices is that their routing paths may be pushed away from their shortest path. In order to reduce the end-to-end delays caused by the stretched routing paths, the model proposed in Chapter 3 introduces the constraints on the length of permitted paths. Another option to address this problem is to only choose from the set of existing shortest paths to transmit data flows. The controller needs to firstly precompute available shortest paths for all pairs of ToR switches that communicate with each other. Then, the controller uses an algorithm to calculate the combination of shortest paths from the precomputed candidates that leads to the energy efficiency. It is worthy of mentioning that this approach has the drawbacks of generating sub-optimal results and computation overhead of calculating shortest paths for all communication pairs. However, network configurations based on precomputed shortest paths can avoid stretched flow paths with excessive long length. More importantly, instead of assigning flows to large number of links, precomputing available flow paths effectively reduces the searching space and computation time. We derive the basic formulation from the model proposed in GreenTE [246] as the baseline to compare with DRL-based solutions.

A directed graph $G = (V, E)$ can be used to represent the topology of a data center network, where $V$ stands for the set of SDN switches and $E$ represents the set of links among them. The k-shortest paths of each communication pair are firstly calculated and denoted by $L_i$. The rest of symbols used in the model are listed in Table 5.1. We formulate the problem as ILP as following.

| Variable | Definition |
|---|---|
| $i :< s_i, r_i, d_i >$ | A tuple of a flow request containing source $s_i$, destination $r_i$ and a bandwidth demand $d_i$ |
| $M$ | A set of flow requests arriving in batches |
| $P_s$ | Static power consumption of the line card, peripheral circuit in a SDN switch |
| $P_o$ | Dynamic power consumption of ports to maintain an activated link |
| $\beta_v$ | $\beta_v = 1$ if the line card and peripheral circuit are activated |
| $\beta_e$ | $\beta_e = 1$ if the ports associated with a link are activated |
| $V$ | A set of SDN switches |
| $E$ | A set of links among SDN switches |
| $L_i$ | A set of precomputed shortest paths for a flow request $i$ |
| $t_l^i$ | $t_l^i = 1$ if a flow request $i$ is assigned onto the path $l$ |
| $\alpha_l^e$ | $\alpha_l^e = 1$ if an edge $e$ belongs to a path $l$ |
| $C$ | Capacity of a link between two SDN switches |

*Table 5.1:* Variables used in the optimization model of DeepGreen.

$$\text{minimize} \quad P_s \sum_{v \in V} \beta_v + P_o \sum_{e \in E} \beta_e / 2 \tag{5.1a}$$

$$\text{subject to} \quad \sum_{l: l \in L_i} t_l^i = 1 \quad , \forall i \in M \tag{5.1b}$$

$$t_l^i \leqslant \beta_v \quad , \forall i \in M, l \in L_i, v \in \text{Nodes}(l) \tag{5.1c}$$

$$t_l^i \leqslant \beta_e \quad , \forall i \in M, l \in L_i, e \in \text{Edges}(l) \tag{5.1d}$$

$$\beta_e = \beta_{e'} \tag{5.1e}$$

$$\sum_i \sum_{l \in L_i} d_i \alpha_l^e t_l^i \leqslant C_e \quad , \forall e \in E, \forall i \in M, \tag{5.1f}$$

$$\alpha_l^e = \begin{cases} 1, \text{if} & e \in l \\ 0, \text{if} & e \notin l \end{cases} \quad , \forall e \in E \tag{5.1g}$$

In this formulation, Constraint (5.1a) is the objective function that sums and minimizes the static and dynamic power of all networking devices in DCN. Constraint (5.1b) indicates that it is allowed to select only one shortest path from all available candidates for a communication request to avoid packet reordering. Constraint (5.1c) and Constraint (5.1d) formalize the condition that the line card, peripheral circuit and ports need to be activated if a switch or a link belongs to a selected shortest path. Constraint (5.1e) indicates that a link

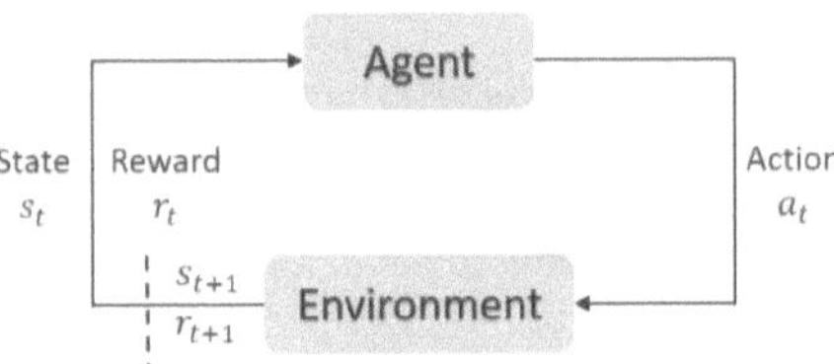


*Figure 5.2:* Concept of reinforcement learning.

transits to sleeping mode when there is no traffic in both up- and down-links. Constraint (5.1f) indicates that the total volume of aggregated workload on a link should not exceed its capacity.

## 5.4 MODEL AND ALGORITHM BASED ON MULTI-AGENT DEEP REINFORCE-MENT LEARNING

In this section, we detail the process of modeling the problem using the deep reinforcement learning approach.

### 5.4.1 *Reinforcement learning*

Reinforcement Learning (RL) is a branch of machine learning, in which an agent interacts with its surrounding environment via a sequence of steps consisting of an observation, an action and a reward [73]. Figure 5.2 depicts the interactions between an agent and environment. In this figure, an *agent* operates in an *environment* characterized by a set of states $s_t \in S$. The agent is capable of choosing an *action* from a set $a_t \in A$. The selection of an action is not performed randomly. Instead, the agent follows a *policy* that is denoted by $\pi(s, a)$ to choose an action. This policy describes the probability of choosing an action $a_t = a$ when facing state $s_t = s$. The agent takes the selected action and receives a reward $r_t$ and receives its new state $s_{t+1}$.

Supervised learning requires a number of samples associated with labels to extract patterns. Instead, RL adopts the approach of trial-and-error to gradually learn actions that can lead to maximum delayed rewards in a dynamic and uncertain environment. This learning process can be described as a Markov Decision Process (MDP). Due to the Markov property (memoryless states), actions selected through a policy only depend on the current states but not the historical ones. The approaches to compute the optimal policy, $\pi's, a,$ are either *model based* or *model free*, depending if a model of the environment is needed or not during training. Agostinelli *et al.* [4] categorize the algorithms to compute the optimal policy into two types: (i) searching first in the space of a *value function* representing the benefit for an agent to reach a given state, then deduce the optimal policy; (ii) representing policies in a explicit way by using a *policy function* and updating it over time. The former category of algorithms includes Linear Programming (LP), Dynamic Programming (DP), Monte-Carlo methods (MC) and Temporal Difference methods (TD). The latter ones include the algorithms based on evolution and Policy Gradient (PG) methods.

### 5.4.2 *Deep reinforcement learning*

Deep learning is fundamentally a representation-learning method that uses multiple levels of simple yet non-linear modules to gradually extract high-level features [130]. It has been successfully applied in resolving various types of engineering problems, ranging from computer vision [24, 140] to network traffic classification [65, 141]. In these applications, deep learning is used as supervised or semi-supervised learning and solved with the stochastic gradient descent algorithm. Neural networks, as the core concept in deep learning, consists of layers of simple, connected neurons being activated by inputs from raw data or other neurons and generating a sequence of real-value outputs. This computation tool is a universal approximator that can *"approximate any measurable function to any desired degree of accuracy"* [100].

Reinforcement learning involves two important functions, namely the value function and the policy function, as briefly introduced above. The idea behind deep reinforcement learning is essentially introducing deep neural networks to represent these two functions. By doing this, it is possible for reinforcement learning algorithms to handle high-dimensional environment and actions. The improvement on one of the classical value-based RL algorithms, Q-learning, can demonstrate this adavantage. In Q-learning, a Q-value is used to represent the goodness of an action under one specific state. The classical Q-learning algorithm uses a table to store and update Q values. However, it is difficult for a Q-value table to represent high-dimensional and continuous states, such as images. Deep Q-learning, and its subsequent extensions, for instance, Double Q-learning [220] use deep neural networks to substitute the Q-value table to assess the maximum reward after carrying out a sequence of actions when observing a complex state.

In contrast to the value-based DRL algorithms, policy-based algorithms directly generate actions and update their policy network. Policy gradient is a typical policy-based algorithm that is effective in high-dimention or continuous action spaces. In the policy gradient approach, the parameters of a policy network are updated by following the policy gradient theorem [207].

More advanced DRL algorithms, such as Deep Deterministic Policy Gradients (DDPG) [137] and Asynchronous Advantage Actor-Critic (A3C) [155] use an actor-critic architecture to combine the advantages of both value-based and policy-based approaches. The actor, which

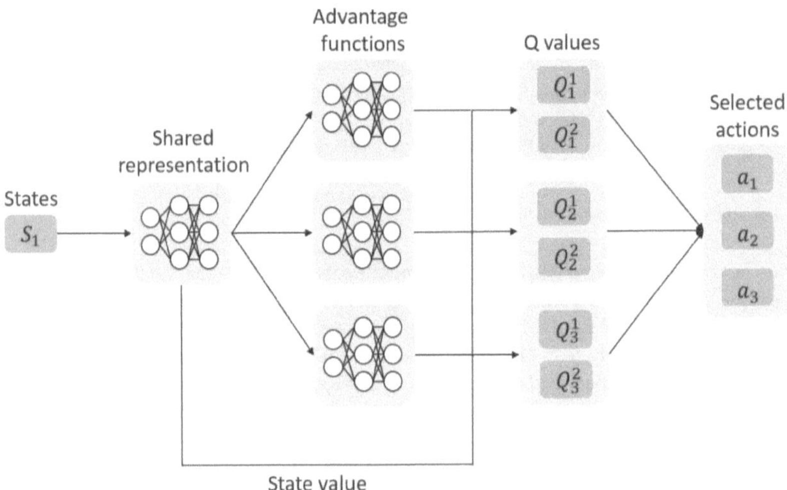


*Figure 5.3:* Illustration of the branching dueling Q-network algorithm.

is policy-based, controls how an agent behaves given the current state of environment. The critic, which is value-based, plays a role of evaluating the situation and the actions selected by the actor. In principle, the goal of updating the parameters of a critic is to make it more accurate in judging the situation and selected actions. The parameters of an actor are updated in the direction indicated by a critic. The expectation on such combination of the value-based and policy-based approaches is that using two models leads to the improvement of the learning efficiency.

### 5.4.3 *DRL-based formulation: algorithm*

In Section 5.4.2, we mention that the commonly used deep reinforcement learning algorithms for optimizing the performance of networks and cloud infrastructures include Deep Q-learning (DQN) [187], DDPG [203] and A3C [235], which are designed for a single agent. More specifically, the controller uses one learning agent to take multiple actions at the same time for the whole network (e.g., assigning link weights). However, from the perspective of each flow, they need to *cooperate* to use power-efficient paths and to achieve low latency of packets. Meanwhile, if we firstly compute all possible combinations of flow paths and take actions on selecting one combination, the total number of combinations is a very large number.

In this contribution, we propose to model the traffic engineering problem using DRL techniques developed for a multi-agent system. Particularly, due to the simplicity and good performance, we choose the Branching Dueling Q-Network algorithm as the base of problem formulation [211]. BDQ is a multi-agent extension of the Deep Duel Q-Network (DDQN) algorithm that is designed to compute sub-actions for one action dimension. Figure 5.3 illustrates the architecture of the BDQ algorithm. The shared representation takes the observed state $S_i$ as the input and produces a corresponding state value that identifies the common part of actions when facing the situation. The advantage values of each dimension of actions is further computed and finally combined with the previously computed state value to calculate the final Q-values for sub-actions in each action dimension. The action associated with the largest Q-value in each action dimension is selected as the output.

### 5.4.4 *DRL-based formulation: modeling*

Section 5.4.1 introduces the vital elements in a model based on deep reinforcement learning, namely states, actions, and rewards. To use the deep reinforcement learning framework to model the scheduling problem of power-efficient DCN, it is necessary to design the corresponding state representation, action space and reward function.

*State representation:* The states that the agent observes are bandwidth demands represented by a serial of traffic matrix. We use $S = \{M_1, M_2, ..., M_k\}$, where $M_i$ is also used in the optimization model described in Section 5.3.2, to denote the sequence of arriving batches of flow requests.

*Action space:* Several experience-driven traffic engineering solutions design the action space in the way that the controller take actions on the link weights. The computed link weights are then utilized to search paths by using shortest path searching algorithms like Dijkstra [59]. In this work, similar to the optimization model, we firstly precompute k candidate shortest paths for each possible communication pair. Afterwards, the controller takes actions on selecting from the precomputed candidate paths and calculates the set of switches and links that need to be activated to construct selected paths. We use $A = \{A_1, A_2, ..., A_i\} = \{\{l_1^1, l_2^1, ..., l_k^1\}, \{l_1^2, l_2^2, ..., l_k^2\}, ..., \{l_1^i, l_2^i, ..., l_k^i\}\}$ to represent the action space consisting of k candidate shortest paths for every flow request i. Hence, the action taken each time is $a = \{l^1, l^2, ..., l^j | l^i \in A_i\}$ and $l^i$ represents one selected shortest path for the flow request i. Comparing with the approaches based on link weights, using precomputed k shortest paths reduces the complexity of the action space and constrains the end-to-end delays caused by stretching flow paths.

The challenge of modelling each flow as one learning agent is that the a large number of concurrently existing agents makes it difficult to collaboratively learn to select appropriate

---

**Algorithm 5** Calculate power consumption of DCN when the controller takes an action

---

**Input:** calculated action $a = \{l^1, l^2, ..., l^j\}$, static power $P_v$, dynamic power $P_o$.
**Output:** power consumption of activated devices $P(a)$.
**Initialize:**
1: $P(a) = 0$

**Main procedure:**
2: **for** $l \in \{l^1, l^2, ..., l^j\}$ **do**
3:     **for** $v \in V$ **do**
4:         **if** $v$ belongs to $l$ **and** $v$ is not marked as active **then**
5:             $P(a) = P(a) + P_v$
6:             Mark $v$ as active
7:         **end if**
8:     **end for**
9:     **for** $e \in E$ **do**
10:         **if** $e$ belongs to $l$ **and** $e$ is not marked as active $v$ is not marked as active **then**
11:             $P(a) = P(a) + P_o$
12:             Mark $e$ and $e'$ as active
13:         **end if**
14:     **end for**
15: **end for**

---

flow paths. Developing DRL algorithms to handle scenarios with many learning agents still remains as a challenge [111]. In order to reduce the number of agents used in the model, the flow requests between $m$ and $n$ in both directions, $< s, r, d > |(s = m, r = n)$ and $< s, r, d > |(s = n, r = m)$, share the decisions made by the same agent. It means that their paths involve the same switches and links but are in the reverse directions.

*Reward function:* The reward considered in this work is the total amount of conserved power consumption when fulfilling incoming communication requests. As a result, the first part of the reward $r$ is $P_r = P_{total} - P(a)$. $P_{total}$ stands for the total power consumption if all devices and links in the network are activated. $P(a)$ is the power consumption that is necessary for keeping devices and links that belong to any selected path in the action $a$. Algorithm 5 provides the details of computing power consumption $P(a)$ of DCN when a controller takes an action. Additionally, as the Constraint (5.1f) of the formal model suggests, the allocated workload on one communication link should not exceed its capacity, otherwise, network congestion happens on this link. To avoid an excessive workload to be assigned to the same link, the designed reward function also includes the experienced delays of packets as the indicator of congestions. Hence, the second part of the reward $r$ is $d$, which is the maximum delay experienced by packets of a flow. To this end, the reward $r$

is represented as $r = P_r - \alpha * d$, where $\alpha$ is the ratio expressing the relative importance of two objectives: reducing power consumption and avoiding link congestion.

## 5.5 EVALUATION

We perform evaluation on the performance of DeepGreen, a DRL-based power optimization method for the software-defined data center networks.

### 5.5.1 Evaluation setups

In order to evaluate our DRL modelling approach, we developed a simulation framework that comprises of a network simulation component implemented with OMNeT++ [168] and a learning component built with a machine learning framework, TensorFlow [213]. These two components interact and share information, such as states (traffic workloads), actions (selection of a shortest path) and rewards (combination of reduced power consumption and pack delays), via the message bus and files.

The time complexity of the training process in the DRL-based power optimization method origins from two aspects: large number of training iterations and relatively slow network simulation. More specifically, the OMNeT++ simulation sequentially processes all transmission events but packet transmission parallelly takes place in reality. As a proof of concept, in order to perform evaluation within reasonable time, the size k of the fat-tree network is set to 4. With this configuration, the total number of switches in the network is 20 and the total number of links among the switches is 32. Each link has two operation modes, namely the active and sleep mode. A link that is configured in the active mode reaches its designed transmission capacity but causes its associated ports, line card and peripheral circuit to consume more power compared with the sleep mode.

The expected workload among edge switches is represented by a traffic matrix $M_i$. Similar to [91], we use a Stride-i traffic model to determine elephant flow entries $M_i$, where an edge switch with id x transmits k data flows to another edge switch with id $(x + i) \mod n$, and n is the total number of edge switches in the network. Additionally, each elephant flow entry in the matrix $M_i$ follows a Markov process that has three states, namely the low date rate, medium date rate and high data rate. The transition probability among these states is defined by the following matrix:

$$
\begin{array}{c}
\text{Current State}
\end{array}
\begin{array}{cc}
 & \text{Next State} \\
\begin{array}{r}
\\
\text{Low} \\
\text{Medium} \\
\text{High}
\end{array} &
\begin{array}{ccc}
\text{Low} & \text{Medium} & \text{High} \\
\left[\begin{array}{ccc}
.5 & .2 & .3 \\
.3 & .4 & .3 \\
.3 & .1 & .6
\end{array}\right]
\end{array}
\end{array}
$$

| Type | Parameter | Configuration |
|---|---|---|
| Network simulator | Topology | K-ary fat tree, K=4 |
| | Capacity of links between core and aggregation switches | 500 Mbit/s |
| | Capacity of links between aggregation and edge switches | 100 Mbit/s |
| | Traffic pattern of a single flow | Poisson distribution |
| | Low, medium, high data rate of a single elephant flow | 20 Mbit/s, 35 Mbit/s, 50 Mbit/s |
| | Power consumption of an active line card | 3 units |
| | Power consumption of an active link | 1 unit |
| Learning algorithm: BDQ | Number of agents | 28 |
| | Number and units of the shared representation layer | 4 x 64 |
| | Number and units of the advantage function layer | 3 x 64 |
| | Number and units of the action layer | 3 x 64 |
| | Exploration factor | 0.1-0.5 |
| | Replay buffer | Experience priority buffer with size of 15000 |
| | Learning rate | 1e-04 |
| | Importance factor of delays | 300 |

*Table 5.2:* Important configurations of the network simulation and reinforcement learning algorithm.

This transition matrix is synthetic but designed so as that the data rate of elephant flow tends to remain unchanged by setting higher self transition probability. The actual transition matrix can be derived from fine granular management data of public clouds owned by corporations such as Microsoft, which is however not publicly available so far [57]. Table 5.2 summarizes the setups and corresponding parameters used in the evaluation.

In this evaluation, we selected two classical approaches to compare with our DeepGreen algorithm. Two classical algorithms are the optimal algorithm and a heuristic algorithm proposed in [242]. The model of the optimal algorithm has been described in Section 5.3.2, and we implement this algorithm by using the Gurobi solver [84]. In the evaluation and training process of DeepGreen, at each step, all algorithms accept the same input data of traffic patterns until the system reward and training process become stable.

### 5.5.2 *Evaluation results and discussion*

We focus on two performance metrics, namely the average normalized power consumption reduction and the average experienced packet delay. The former one is calculated by dividing the number of power consumption reduction measured in units with the total number of power consumption if all devices and links are activated. The latter one represents the maximum value of the average delays experienced by packets of all flows in the network. It represents the congestion level in the network since the current implementation of the simulation model does not include propagation delays and processing delays on links and switches.

#### 5.5.2.1 *Summary of results*

Figure 5.4 shows the evolution of the system performance metrics during the training process of DeepGreen and the corresponding results of the optimal and heuristic algorithms. Figure 5.5 shows the performance of different algorithms within the last 100 steps when the training becomes stable.

Particularly, Figure 5.4a depicts the average normalized power consumption reduction during the training process. This figure shows that the training process of DeepGreen starts from the states where the flow paths are dispersed. It is the opposite of the state where the flows are consolidated and the power conservation is maximized. As the training continues, the percent of reduced power consumption increases until there is almost no further improvement. Compared with the average 26% power consumption reduction achieved by the optimal and heuristic algorithms, DeepGreen achieves around 25% of their performance in this major network optimization goal, as shown in Figure 5.5a.

Figure 5.4b shows the average experienced delays of flow packets across the training epochs of DeepGreen. In this figure and Figure 5.5b, DeepGreen maintains relatively

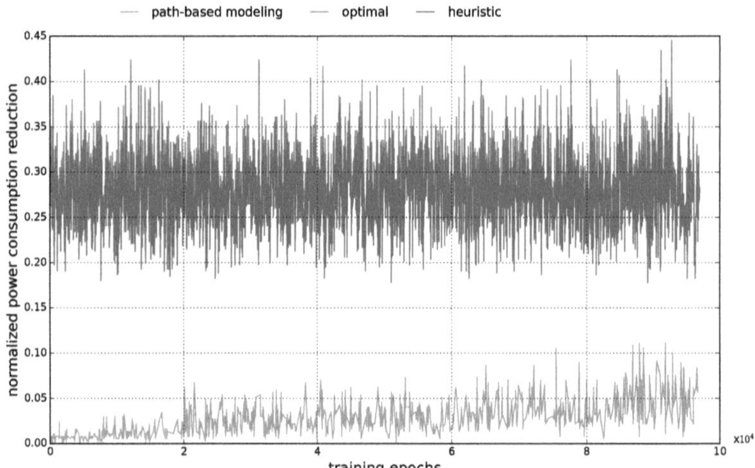

(a) Average normalized power consumption reduction when training DeepGreen.

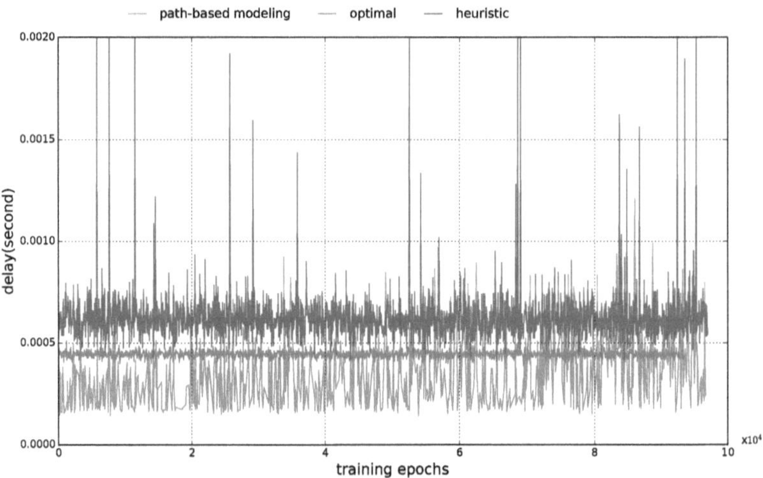

(b) Average delays experienced by flow packets during training DeepGreen.

*Figure 5.4:* Performance comparison with the optimal and heuristic algorithms when training Deep-Green.

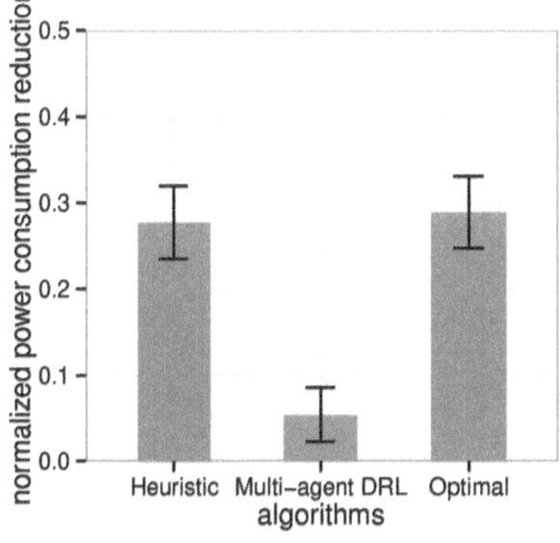

(a) Average normalized power consumption reduction within the last 100 steps when the training becomes stable.

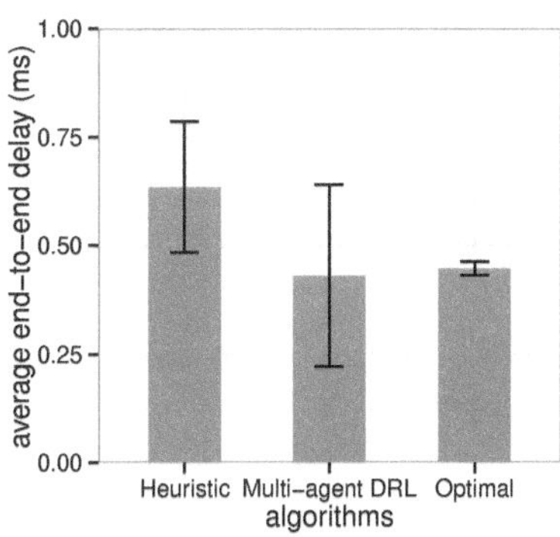

(b) Average delays experienced by flow packets within the last 100 steps when the training becomes stable.

*Figure 5.5:* Performance comparison with the optimal and heuristic algorithms after the training becomes stable.

low delays (with an average below 0.0005 second) compared with the heuristic algorithm, although the delays are volatile. It is because that the during the training process, there is a chance that a path is selected randomly for exploration. We can also see from Figure 5.4b, that the optimal solution leads to the minimum delays due to the strict constraints on the maximum allowed aggregated data rates on each link. It is also worthy of noticing that the energy-efficient heuristic algorithm causes link congestions, which are indicated by those spikes, from time to time. It is due to its greedy searching strategy for the paths that lead to the maximum level of flow aggregation.

### 5.5.2.2 *Discussion of evaluation results*

Classical algorithms are able to solve the problem of reducing the power consumption of SDN-based computer networks through flow consolidation. Deep reinforcement learning has achieved great success in many tasks. But it is a challenging task to directly apply the DRL approach to perform power conservation under the setups and assumptions presented in this chapter, which is confirmed by the simulation results. This is due to: (i) the open challenges when deep reinforcement learning is applied to solve a complex task [111]; (ii) the unique properties of the setups and assumptions of the problem addressed by this chapter. We discuss possible factors that play vital roles in determining the performance of the DRL-based formulation for the power conservation problem investigated in this chapter.

- Sparse rewards. The current power model of forwarding devices requires that a device or a link can be put into the sleep mode when they do not host any flow, which is a relatively strict precondition. As a result, when a learning agent explores other alternative paths to place a flow, redirecting one flow from a specific device or link is not sufficient to trigger the operation of power conservation and to improve the reward signal, until the last one is removed. On the contrary, some other optimization objectives, such as reducing end-to-end delays, are very sensitive to the change of flow routing paths, which makes this reward signal dynamic. In fact, the additional evaluation presented in Appendix A.1 shows that, our multi-agent DRL formulation performs better in the task of reducing end-to-end delays (27% improvement) compared with the task of conserving network power consumption (7% improvement). Dealing with sparse rewards is still a challenge for current deep reinforcement learning algorithms [111].

- Large action dimension. The action dimension, that equals to the number of communication pairs in the DeepGreen formulation or the number of connections in the link-weight based formulation, is large compared with the typical setups used in the deep reinforcement learning community. In the formulation based on the multi-agent paradigm, each agent represents one action dimension and they try to achieve a high reward in a collaborative way. Even with mechanisms that support communicating information of other agents' actions, such as the shared representation in BDQ and the centralized critic in MADDPG [142], it is still difficult for a single agent to correctly update its gradients when facing the highly dynamic environment.

- Coexisting traffic engineering objectives. In this work, the reward function is designed as the weighted sum of two objectives: conserving power consumption and avoiding link congestion. These two objectives contradict with each other since power conservation requires flow consolidation and congestion avoidance requires flow dissemination. But these two objectives are not strictly in a inverse relation under the current assumptions. For example, migrating a flow from one link to alleviate the congestion does not necessarily increase the power consumption due to the definition of the assumed power model. Hence, it is also a challenge to correctly update gradients of each agent without advanced techniques developed for multi-objective DRL [164].

Based on the above discussion, it is possible to further improve the performance of the DRL-based formulation for the presented power conservation problem from the following aspects.

First of all, a model with finer granularity of power changes depending on the assigned traffic workload provides dense reward signals. Instead of assuming only two operation modes, active mode and sleep mode, for network devices, an adaptive power model that dynamically calculates power consumption depending on the aggregated workload on each link and devices. More specifically, we can use a linear or non-linear function to precisely describe the relation between the power-consumption and device workload, so as to increase the density of reward signals.

Secondly, it is important to understand the stability of different DRL algorithms in multi-agent and multi-objective scenarios. For example, the link-weight-based formulation used in the algorithm comparison relies on the DDPG algorithm, which struggles in achieving balance between the power reduction and congestion mitigation in our experiment. Comparing with the typical evaluation scenarios reported in literature where state-of-the-art DRL algrithms are proposed, the scale of network optimization problems is larger in terms of the number of agents or the number of actions. The capability of newly developed DRL algorithms that handle complex multi-agent and multi-objective network traffic engineering problem requires investigation by extensive evaluation.

## 5.6 RELATED WORK

The recent breakthroughs, including hardware accelerators and algorithm advances, of deep learning has boosted the development of many autonomous and intelligent systems. As a result, deep learning based network management, such as intelligent network traffic control systems, has recently received attentions and been developed to optimize the performance of data networks and cloud infrastructures [65]. In [167], deep learning is used to explore time-varying properties of network workloads and to perform network traffic prediction for data centers. The authors of [146] show that local switches can use supervised learning based on Artificial Neural Networks (ANN) to learn the routing strategies taken by previous data packets or generated by traditional routing protocols. The routing decisions are computed through inferences instead of using the signaling mechanism that commonly exists in routing protocols like OSPF. Similar work such as [255] also relies on the empirical traffic routing data and an ANN-based sequence-to-sequence model to learn appropriate data paths with certain constraints.

Deep reinforcement learning becomes attractive in optimizing network performance due to its capability of being self-adaptive and being trained without a data set that is necessary for supervised learning. The authors of the pioneer work [203, 235] adapt the classical DRL algorithms such as DDPG and A3C to learn how to arrange paths for data flows to achieve low latencies. The output actions in these work are the weight of network links. DeepConf [187] is a DRL-based network topology management framework for hybrid data center networks comprised of wired, wireless or free optical links. It accepts traffic matrix as the current state and computes augmented network topologies that lead to maximum link utilization and minimum flow completion time. In addition to the flow scheduling problem, DRL-based approaches are also used in many aspects of modern network and cloud systems. For example, DRL-based approaches are able to control the cooling system of data centers to reduce power consumption [136], calculate strategies of task offloading and radio resource assignment in edge computing [53] or dynamically adjust allocated resources to embed virtual networks in a cloud [152].

## 5.7 CONCLUSION

In this chapter, we investigate the question that if the multi-agent deep reinforcement learning technique can improve networking power efficiency. To this end, we developed a DRL-based optimization framework named DeepGreen, which includes a multi-agent DRL formulation based on actions of selection from shortest paths for each data flow. Evaluation results show that the classical algorithms still can achieve the best performance and our developed DRL-based formulation can achieve power reduction to some extent while maintaining relatively low delays. Compared with the link-weight-based DRL formulation, the modeling approach in DeepGreen can achieve similar power efficiency but better control of experienced packet delays. Furthermore, we discussed the possible directions to improve the performance of our proposed DRL-based formulation for this particular problem.

CHAPTER 6

# MITIGATE ABUSIVE USAGE OF SDN CONTROL PLANE RESOURCE

## 6.1 INTRODUCTION

The resource conservation models and algorithms developed in the previous chapters run in a centralized network controller. The responsiveness of the implemented network configuration modules to react to incoming communication requests depends on the efficiency of proposed algorithms, as well as on the availability of resources used to perform computation and transmission of control messages. Section 2.3.3 introduces a very harmful, yet easy to implement, Denial of Service attack that misuses the separation between the control plane and data plane is the CPS *attack*. CPS is a general problem for the centralized software-defined networking technology. In software-defined radio, saturation of the cognitive control channel is implemented by sending a large amount of cognitive messages [15]. Since we perform network configurations mainly using traffic engineering supported by centralized software-defined network management, this chapter focuses on CPS taking place in OpenFlow-based SDN.

In OpenFlow-based SDN, switches and routers[1] in SDN are devices that are responsible only of forwarding traffic according to the decisions taken by a (logically) centralized network controller. In DoS attacks targeting SDN, the adversary exploits the fact that SDN switches send control packets to the controller whenever their flow tables miss rules matching for incoming flow packets. In particular, the adversary generates a large number of such packets rapidly. This will trigger the switches to flood both the controller and the control channels with control packets with the malicious intention of tearing down the control plane. The malicious control packets will consume the computational resources of the controller as well as the bandwidth of the control plane. As a consequence, the communication between the switches and the controller will be disrupted, and the legitimate flow packets will not be (timely) handled.

As already summarized in Section 2.3.3, many proposed solutions are commonly implemented as protection modules on the controller side [61, 191, 224, 227]. The protection module receives incoming control packets, before other controller modules, and analyzes them to identify potential adversaries (those generating flow packets that cause large

---

1 From now onward, the term *switch* will represent both types of devices.

amounts of control packets). Once potential adversaries are identified, the protection module carries out some mitigation actions (e.g., installing flow rules in the switches to block traffic coming from the identified hosts [224]). While these solutions are effective in protecting the computational resources of the controller, they do not alleviate the bandwidth saturation in the control plane. This is because all control packets still have to be sent from the switches to the controller untill they are handled by the protection module.

In this chapter, we present a solution – **In-Network Flow mAnagement Scheme** (INFAS) – to protect SDN networks against CPS. INFAS addresses the aforementioned drawbacks of prior solutions by a *self-contained in-network* module to handle the malicious data flows from a source, before they saturate the control plane. INFAS is designed as a network function running on the commodity servers installed near network switches. Such in-network resources are already available in the current, rapidly increasing, networks that support Network Functionality Virtualization. Switches send flow packets that do not match any rule in their flow tables firstly to INFAS for evaluation. INFAS, in turn, employs a novel threshold-based algorithm to determine the probability of allowing the received flow packets to return to the switches and trigger the corresponding control packets. To reduce the delay caused by this additional processing step, we build INFAS using the Data Plane Development Kit (DPDK) [104]. We evaluate the effectiveness of INFAS extensively through a representative prototype and network emulations.

The remainder of the chapter is structured as follows: we motivate and describe the design of INFAS in Section 6.2. The evaluation results are presented in Section 6.3. Section 6.4 provides additional summary of related work, and we conclude this chapter in Section 6.5.

## 6.2 OUR SOLUTION:INFAS

In this section, we first motivate this design choice, then describe INFAS, our solution for protecting SDN against the CPS DoS attacks.

### 6.2.1 *Motivation for proactive in-network protection*

Installing protection modules in the SDN controller has been shown to be a working approach to protect SDN against resource saturation. This is mainly because the controller, as a central network management entity, has a global view of control and flow packets. With such a view, the protection module can, for example, precisely evaluate the trustworthiness of flow senders [227]. The controller workload can be alleviated, for example, by buffering incoming control packets [227] or by offloading the workload to other resources [223].

Nevertheless, even with this improvement, the controller-based protection approach cannot timely mitigate the bandwidth saturation of the control channel (resulting from

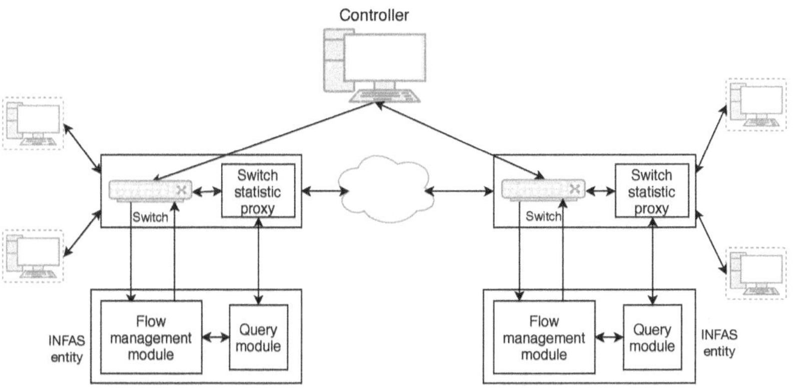


*Figure 6.1:* The system architecture of INFAS.

excessive amounts of control packets – see Section 2.3.3.1). Furthermore, to enable adaptivity in the controller-based approach, the controller is required to frequently acquire flow statistics from the switches and to update their flow tables accordingly. This translates into additional large amounts of control packets, and subsequently into bandwidth saturation. Event the approaches using in-network caches of control packets [223] suffer the delay between the switch and controller. Last but not the least, the Open Flow Agent (OFA) in the switch is only capable of generating limited number of `packet_in` messages, due to the CPU constraint [247]. Thus, the overloaded switch OFA under DoS attack can also cause the switch to delay or drop the packets from benign entities.

Motivated by the latest trend of deploying virtualised network functions in the network to achieve network management tasks, we argue that it is a new approach to offload the CPS protection to self-contained in-network modules running in a SDN network. By doing this, both the switch and the control plane resources, including the computation and bandwidth resources, are preserved. The responsiveness of a protection scheme to mitigate CPS is also improved.

### 6.2.2  *Architecture design*

Figure 6.1 depicts a SDN network deployed with INFAS. For each switch, we deploy an INFAS instance on a connected server. In this chapter, we do not consider cooperation, thus there is no communication, among INFAS instances. Each INFAS instance consists of three components: (i) a flow management module, (ii) a query module, and (iii) a switch statistic proxy. In the following, we describe each of these components, and how they interact with each other.

The *flow management module* accepts the flow packets that do not hit any flow rule. It includes an attack detection and a mitigation algorithm performing analysis over statistics collected from both unmatched flow packets and the query module. It determines the severity of control plane saturation caused by the packets from a flow source. Accordingly, the flow management module tunes action parameters for each suspicious entity, e.g., a host or a port, to drop a portion of the corresponding unmatched flow packets. Other unmatched flow packets are considered legitimate, and they are sent back to the switch via another port and will trigger packet_in messages.

The *query module* is responsible for collecting information that cannot be directly derived by the flow management module. This information includes basic flow statistics, such as flow packet counters. The query module requests them, at regular time intervals, from the switch statistic proxy. Once the information is collected, the query module sends them to the flow management module. The flow management module is separated from the query module, i.e. they work asynchronously, because the former is tasked to perform in-network packet processing at a high speed, while the latter involves slow I/O operations, such as socket communication.

The *switch statistic proxy* is a small piece of code that runs in the switch to bridge the switch with the two other INFAS components. As described above, the switch statistic proxy receives inquiries from the query module asking for flow statistics. To answer these inquiries, the switch statistic proxy executes basic switch control commands, aggregates the returned results, and lastly sends the aggregated results back to the query module.


### 6.2.3 *Flow rule design*

To support the detection and mitigation algorithm, INFAS defines three categories of flow rules: (i) concrete flow rule, (ii) redirection flow rule, and (iii) monitoring flow rule. We illustrate the roles of these categories through an example. In the example, there is a switch s1 with four ports: port 0 is an egress port used to send flow packets to the flow management module, port 1 is an ingress port used to receive data from the same module, port 2 is connecting s1 with a host h1 with the IP address 10.0.0.1, and port 3 which a output port for flow packets. Table 6.1 shows four exemplary flow rules following INFAS design.

The *concrete flow rules* perform exact matching for packet flows, to achieve the actual goal of some network control logic (e.g. routing). The controller is responsible for installing these rules in the switches' flow tables. In the example, rule 1 is a concrete flow rule that specifies the output port 3 for the flow packets having the source IP address 10.0.0.1

| Flow rule | Category | Table ID | Src IP | Dst IP | Priority | In_port | Action |
|---|---|---|---|---|---|---|---|
| Rule 1 | Concrete | 0 | 10.0.0.1 | 10.0.0.2 | 2 | 2 (h1 – s1) | Output:3 & GOTO Table 1 |
| Rule 2 | Redirection | 0 | * | * | 1 | 2 (h1 – s1) | Output: 0 |
| Rule 3 | Monitoring | 1 | 10.0.0.1 | * | 1 | 2 (h1 – s1) | None |
| Rule 4 | Implicit | * | * | * | 1 | * | Controller |

*Table 6.1:* Exemplary INFAS flow rules.

and the destination IP address 10.0.0.2. From now onward, we will use the terms *matched packets* and *unmatched packets* to respectively refer to the flow packets that match and those that do not match concrete flow rules.

The purpose of the *redirection flow rules* is to avoid sending packet_in messages from the switch to the controller in the case of unmatched packets. In the current INFAS design, unmatched packets are simply forwarded to the INFAS flow management module. Rule 2 is an exemplary redirection flow rule that specifies the output port 0 for the unmatched packets that arrive through port 2. Note that it is possible to select a portion of unmatched packets using more specific matching fields, depending on the concrete flow rules. Redirection flow rules always have lower priority than concrete flow rules, which assures that flow packets first obey the network control logic.

The *monitoring flow rules* are intended to help to obtain basic statistics, like the number of matched packets received from a host or through a port. These rules are usually installed in the flow table (e.g. flow table 1) following the one containing concrete flow rules and redirection flow rules (e.g. flow table 0). In the example, rule 3 is a monitoring flow rule that counts the total number of matched packets coming from h1, since all packets matching rule 1 are forced to go through the flow rule table 1.

In the example, rule 4 is the default flow rule. A flow packet that is permitted by INFAS to return to the switch will not match any flow rule belonging to the above three categories. Because of the default flow rule, the returned packet will ultimately incur a table-miss event.

### 6.2.4 *Flow management algorithm*

Many DoS mitigation algorithms in SDN tend to clearly distinguish between malicious flows and legitimate flows. They subsequently block the sources of potentially malicious flows. A widely used approach is to use the amount of triggered control packets as a detection parameter. However, we argue that this approach can be inaccurate. This is because a large number of control packets can be attributed to legitimate flow packets originating from a source during a workload peak. Instead, we propose a threshold-based flow management algorithm that does not block a network entity completely.

As shown in Figure 6.2, the algorithm identifies four different control plane's saturation severity levels. Accordingly, the algorithm applies distinct mitigation strategies on incoming unmatched packets.

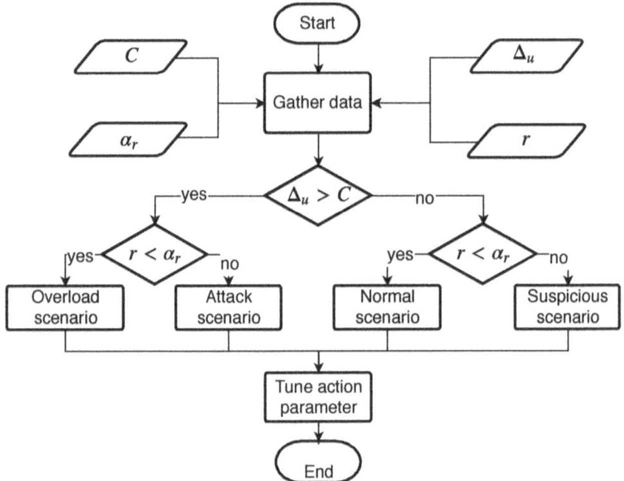


*Figure 6.2:* INFAS flow management algorithm.

The algorithm executes in a periodic manner, for instance, every one second. It uses two input thresholds: (i) the packet_in budget C and (ii) the threshold of unmatched packets proportion $\alpha_r$. The first threshold defines, within a time slot, the maximum number of flow packets permitted to trigger packet_in messages. It highly depends on the capacity of the controller and the expected number of networking entities sending packet flows. A simple method to determine the budget value is to divide the controller capacity among the network entities. The second threshold specifies the maximum allowed percentage of unmatched flow packets received from a host or port. To measure the unmatched packet proportion, the algorithm uses the unmatched and matched packet statistics, $\Delta_u$ and $\Delta_m$, respectively collected from the flow management module and the query module. The unmatched packet proportion for a network entity is: $r = \Delta_u/(\Delta_u + \Delta_m)$.

The algorithm uses the above-described input values to calculate the *acceptance probability* p, that is defined as the probability to return an unmatched packet to the switch. In principle, the more severe the saturation caused by a network entity, the smaller the acceptance probability p for the corresponding flow packets.

In the following, we describe the four severity levels, and the corresponding categorization conditions and p values:

- *Normal case* ($\Delta_u < C, r < \alpha_r$): Here, the amount of unmatched packets is less than the packet_in budget, and majority of flow packets received from a network entity can hit the concrete flow rules. The algorithm allows all unmatched packets to return to the switch and trigger table-miss events. The acceptance probability p in this case is set to 1.

- *Suspicious case* ($\Delta_u < C, r > \alpha_r$): We consider this case as suspicious because these packets do not bring much workload to the control plane, although a relatively large portion of flow packets received from the network entity trigger table-miss events. In this case, the algorithm introduces a small penalty, according to which only a small portion of the unmatched packets are dropped: $p = 1 - \tanh(r * 2)$, in which tanh is a hyperbolic tangent function.

- *Overload case* ($\Delta_u > C, r < \alpha_r$): Under these conditions, the control plane is considered overloaded, because the number of unmatched packets exceeds the packet_in budget. Meanwhile, majority of the flow packets can match the concrete flow rules. This can be interpreted as a workload peak. In this case, the algorithm simply regulates the rate of unmatched packets to be the same as the budget value: $p = C/\Delta_u$.

- *Attack case* ($\Delta_u > C, r > \alpha_r$): This is the most severe case. More precisely, the amount of unmatched packets exceeds the packet_in budget, and the network entity sends a large amount of flow packets that will trigger packet_in messages. This case is very likely caused by an attack. To mitigate the aggressive impact of the attack on the control plane, the algorithm dramatically decreases the acceptance probability: $p = C/\Delta_u * (1 - \tanh(r * 10))$.

## 6.3 IMPLEMENTATION AND EVALUATION

In this section, we detail our implementation and evaluation. We first describe INFAS prototype implementation and the evaluation setup, then discuss the evaluation results.

### 6.3.1 *Implementation highlights*

Redirecting flow packets to be firstly examed by our INFAS entity is an *on-the-path* solution, in which additional processing takes place during packet forwarding. In order to reduce the additional intermediate processing delay caused by the INFAS entity, we use the Intel's Data Plane Development Kit (DPDK) framework [104] to accelerate packet processing.

DPDK is a framework supporting the development of virtualized network functions that run on off-the-shelf hosts equipped with CPUs. It takes the advantage of modern multi-core CPUs to parallelize packets of processing so as to reduce the queuing delays. Network functions developed with DPDK directly fetch incoming packets by polling the network card and passing through the Linux network stack. This mechnism further reduces processing delays experienced by packets. This implementation choice provides the required performance guarantees for fast in-network packet processing [124]. It also enables to integrate INFAS into a DPDK-based NFV platforms, such as openNetVM [102, 250].

The flow management module and the query module are both implemented as DPDK applications. The query module exchanges information with the flow management module through a high-speed ring buffer provided by DPDK. The query module also communicates with the switch statistic proxy using standard TCP/IP sockets. Both the flow management module and the query module run on a Netgate DPDK box [153], containing a Quad Core Intel(R) Atom(TM) E3845 1.91 GHz CPU and 2GB RAM.

We use one Open vSwtich (OvS) instance [169] as the SDN switch in the experiment. As for the switch statistic proxy, it is implemented as a Python script running on the same host as the OvS. To query the flow statistics, the switch statistic proxy interacts with the OvS using OvS-Python APIs [172].

### 6.3.2 *Evaluation setup*

#### 6.3.2.1 *Testbed scenario*

Our evaluations are based on a testbed emulating the functionality of a SDN-based server workload balancer. As illustrated in Figure 6.3, the testbed consists of a Floodlight [72] controller, an OvS s1 protected by an INFAS instance, and three hosts {h1, h2, h3} running as Docker containers [60]. The host h1 has the IP address 192.168.0.1, which represents an external entity. The hosts h2 and h3 are internal servers assigned with the IP addresses 10.0.0.2 and 10.0.0.3, respectively. To expose the service to the outside world, h2 and h3 also share an external IP address 192.168.0.20. The OvS and the three containers run on a machine equipped with a four-core Intel(R) Core(TM) i5-6500 CPU and 32GB RAM.

In the experiments, h1 sends packet flows, from its socket ports, to different ports belonging to 192.168.0.20. The role of s1 is to evenly distribute the flow packets from h1

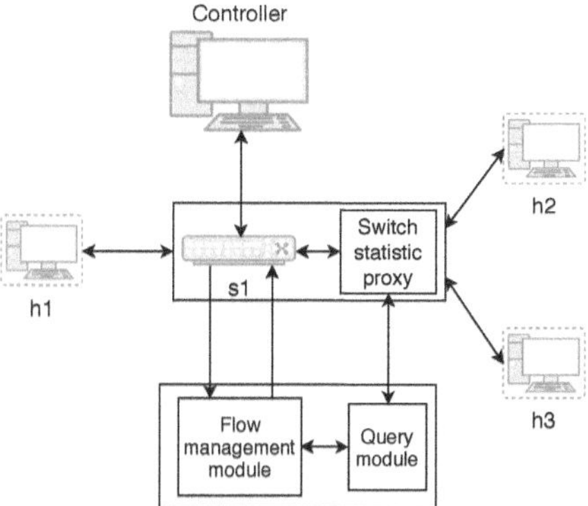


*Figure 6.3:* Setups of the testbed.

to the servers {h2, h3}, by mapping their IP addresses and ports. s1 performs a four-tuple {Source IP, Source port, Destination IP, Destination port} matching. For example, when h1 sends packets to 192.168.0.20:1, according to the concrete flow rule in s1, the destination IP address 192.168.0.20 is converted to an internal IP address (10.0.0.2 or 10.0.0.3), and the port number 1 is mapped to a new port number (e.g. 10). After this conversion, the packets are sent to the corresponding server. When an internal server replies with flow packets to h1, the source IP address is converted back to 192.168.0.20.

The above-described mapping procedure is managed by the controller. In particular, the controller decides which server and which port are mapped for a flow coming from h1, upon receiving the packet_in messages. For each flow, the controller installs flow rules specifying an output port, and rewrites the packet's destination IP address and destination port. Each concrete flow rule is configured with an idle timeout of 2 seconds, to reduce the number of concrete flow rules.

### 6.3.2.2 *Launching the CPS attack*

An aggressive CPS attack is emulated by a script running in h1. More precisely, the script generates a large number of unmatched packets from h1 to 192.168.0.20 using 2000 different destination ports. As we already described in Section 4.5, if the packet inter-arrival time of a flow exceeds the idle timeout (2s in this experiment), a large number of packet_in messages are generated. Particularly, we define two types of flows, namely *normal flows* and *abnormal flows*. The packet intervals of normal flows and abnormal flows follows the exponential and gaussian distribution correspondingly. It is a common practice in network simulations to assume a Poisson process to generate data packets [29]. The parameter

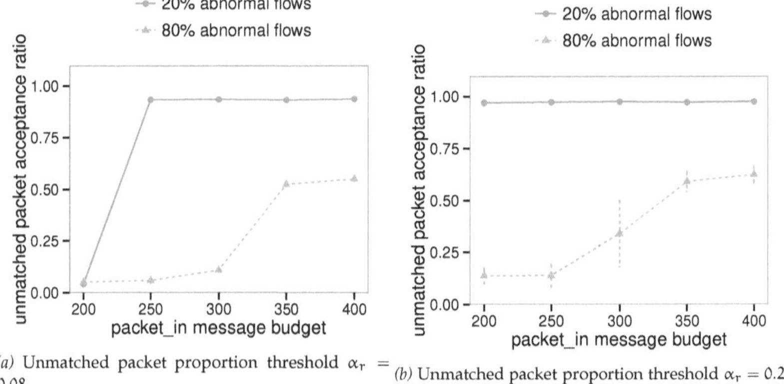


(a) Unmatched packet proportion threshold $\alpha_r = 0.08$.    (b) Unmatched packet proportion threshold $\alpha_r = 0.2$.

*Figure 6.4:* INFAS performance when packet_in message budget C varies.

lamda of a exponential distribution is configured as 0.4. The intervals of abnormal flows follow a Gaussian distribution with the mean value of 2.5 and standard deviation of 0.5. By varying the ratio between the number of the abnormal and normal flows, we could emulate different severity of CPS attacks. In the experiments, we call this parameter as the *abnormal flow percentage.*

### 6.3.2.3 *Evaluation metrics and focused parameters*

We use two system performance metrics: (i) the measured unmatched packet acceptance ratio $R_{accep}$ and (ii) the switch throughput. The first metric enables to evaluate the mitigation effectiveness of INFAS against the CPS attack. $R_{accep} = n_c/n_i$, where $n_c$ is the number of unmatched packets that finally trigger generation of packet_in messages measured at the controller, and $n_i$ is the number of unmatched packets forwarded to INFAS. As for the switch throughput, it is obtained by measuring the experienced bandwidth between two hosts connected with the protected switch. We use this metric to show that INFAS is able to reduce the workload of the protected switch. In order to evaluate the impact of the system parameters, we experiment with varying packet_in budget C values and varying unmatched packet proportion thresholds $\alpha_r$.

### 6.3.3 Results

We conduct two sets of experiments to measure the unmatched packet acceptance ratio. In the first set, we fix the unmatched packet proportion threshold $\alpha_r \in \{0.08, 0.2\}$, and vary the packet_in budget C from 200 to 400. In the second group, we fix $C \in \{200, 400\}$, and vary $\alpha_r$ from 0.02 to 0.26. In both sets of experiments, we experiment with two different CPS attack severity levels: (i) light CPS with 20% abnormal flows and (ii) severe CPS with 80% abnormal flows.

#### 6.3.3.1 Impact of the packet_in message budget

Figure 6.4 depicts the impact of the packet_in budget C. In particular, Figure 6.4a shows INFAS performance under different packet_in budgets, when $\alpha_r$ is fixed to 0.08. We can see that, in the light CPS case, $R_{accep}$ remains small when only a small number of packet_in messages (less than 250) are allowed to be generated within a time slot. After that, it increases dramatically since the increased packet_in message budget is sufficient to process incoming control messages. As for the severe CPS case, the acceptance ratio $R_{accep}$ always remains below 0.25 when the packet_in message budget is below 350. This means that INFAS blocks the majority of unmatched packets from h1 and it is classified as an attack case. Even when the packet_in message budget increases, almost half of unmatched packets are blocked and it is classified as an overload case.

Figure 6.4b shows the system performance when $\alpha_r$ is fixed to 0.2. We can see that, due to the large control message budget and great tolerance on the proportion of unmatched packets, the light attacks are ignored. In the case of severe attacks, it is similar to the results shown by Figure 6.4a, but with slightly higher unmatched packet acceptance ratio because that the unmatched packet proportion threshold $\alpha_r$ is relatively large.

These results can be commented as follows: in the light CPS case, the proportion of unmatched packets is relatively small and just a bit lower than the threshold $\alpha_r$. The flow management algorithm treats it as an attack case when $\alpha_r$ is very small. Otherwise it is classified as a normal or suspicious case, thus INFAS enforces a light penalty. However, in the severe CPS case, a large portion of packets from h1 cannot match concrete flow rules due to their long inter-arrival time. The flow management algorithm classifies it as an attack case or overload case, thus enforces a heavy penalty on the acceptance probability p.

#### 6.3.3.2 Impact of the unmatched packet proportion threshold

Figure 6.5 depicts the impact of the unmatched packet proportion threshold $\alpha_r$ on INFAS performance. Figure 6.5a shows the performance change under different values of $\alpha_r$, when C is fixed to 200. In general, we can see that increasing $\alpha_r$ allows INFAS to let more unmatched packets to trigger table-miss events. In the light CPS case, $R_{accep}$ is small (less than 0.5) when $\alpha_r$ is set to 0.02 and 0.08, and it starts to become constant once $\alpha_r$ reaches a

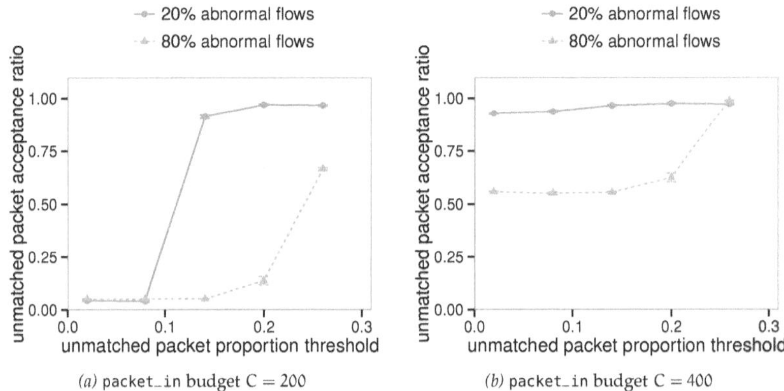


(a) packet_in budget $C = 200$      (b) packet_in budget $C = 400$

*Figure 6.5:* INFAS performance under varying unmatched packet proportion thresholds $\alpha_r$

certain value. The reason is that when $\alpha_r$ is large enough, the light CPS case will be treated as an normal case by the flow management algorithm.

Figure 6.5b shows that, in the configuration of large control message budgets, changing threshold $\alpha_r$ can cause sudden changes in the result. The change of $\alpha_r$ has a similar effect on the system performance in the severe CPS case, when C is set both to 200 and to 400. More precisely, the resulting unmatched packet acceptance ratio remains low but stable for some threshold values, but may increase suddenly when the threshold $\alpha_r$ is beyond 0.2.

With the above presented results, we confirm that INFAS can effectively block malicious flow packets that deliberately trigger table-miss events in SDN networks. By this, INFAS significantly mitigates CPS, depending on the severity level of the attack. Meanwhile, it is worthy of noticing that changing the value of packet_in message budget leads to smoother transition of classified cases. But changing the value of the unmatched packet proportion threshold $\alpha_r$ leads to more dramatic changes of the system performance. In addition, choosing proper values for C and $\alpha_r$ in real systems requires to measure the controller capacity and to estimate the traffic patterns. When this is achieved, INFAS parameters can be tuned in an adaptive way. Such system extensions and improvements are among our agenda for future work.

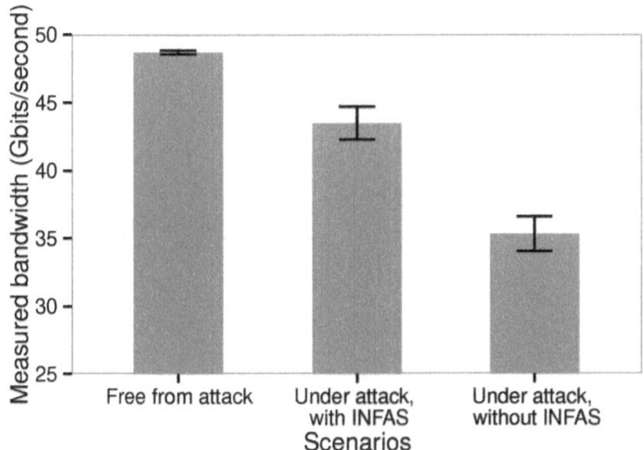


*Figure 6.6:* Performance of the SDN switch

### 6.3.3.3 *Switch throughput*

We measure the switch throughput by connecting an additional pair of Docker containers to s1, and configuring several static concrete flow rules to allow their mutual communication. In our evaluation, we consider the measured bandwidth between this pair of containers as the throughput of the switch. The standard tool iperf3 [107] is used to test the bandwidth.

Figure 6.6 shows the measured switch throughput under three scenarios: (i) attack-free system, (ii) a system under a severe CPS attack with INFAS enabled, and (iii) a system under a severe CPS attack without INFAS. Note that, due to the fact that OvS operates in the kernel mode, its throughput can reach about 47 Gbit/s on the used hardware. Other results can be summarized as follows: under the severe CPS attack without protection, the switch throughput drops to around 35 Gbit/s. When enabling INFAS, we achieve roughly 44 Gbit/s. Such an improvement (about 26%) confirms that INFAS effectively blocks a large amounts of unmatched packets before they trigger the generation of packet_in messages. More accurately, the workload of the switch CPU and the netlink channel connecting the OvS kernel module and the OpenFlow daemon is dramatically reduced, which contributes to the improved switch performance.

## 6.4 RELATED WORK

The aforementioned controller-based solutions in Section 2.3.3.1 do not alleviate the bandwidth consumption caused by the exchanged control packets. That is, the control requests (i.e. packet_in messages) will be sent from the switches to the controller, and their responses will be sent in the opposite direction, until the protection module deals with them. The size of each `packet_in` message is around 160 bytes. In the case that the arrival rate of the `packet_in` messages from one switch in the network is $10^4$ per second, the overall consumed bandwidth of the control plane is 1.6 kB/s. In order to compute the overall bandwidth consumption along the control path, we can further multiply this value with the distance (measured in hops) from a switch to the controller. Additionally, due to the propagation delay between a switch and the controller, the solutions residing on the controller side can only detect abnormality after receiving `packet_in` messages.

Some prior works also implement the in-network approach, to some extent. For instance, the authors of [14], aiming to protect the so-called operational environment, propose to duplicate that environment in a sandbox. The unmatched flow packets coming from the operational environment are firstly sent to the switches in the sandbox network. The controller and the switches in the sandbox follow the regular flow handling procedure. After a certain timeout interval, the flow rules that remain in the flow tables of the sandbox switches are considered safe. These rules are installed into the flow tables of the corresponding switches in the operational environment. However, the control plane in the sandbox network still faces the DoS attack, and the flows suffer processing delay due to the time waited to confirm the flow rules.

Two other notable in-network solutions are FloodGuard [223] and AVANT-GUARD [195]. FloodGuard employs symbolic executions to pre-generate flow rules to increase the responsiveness of the controller. It further uses in-network packet queues to cache all unmatched flow packets. FloodGuard translates the cached flow packets into control packets in a round-robin way based on protocol types, and sends them to a migration agent running inside the controller. As for AVANT-GUARD, it aims to prevent TCP-based DoSS attacks, using additional modules introduced into the design of the switch architecture. Its principle idea is to allow only the flow packets arriving from a source that can complete a TCP handshake to trigger `packet_in` messages.

The above discussed in-network solutions either still implement the mitigation logic in the controller (like [14, 223]), or are hard to implement (like [195] which requires to change the switch architecture). In contrast, INFAS implements the mitigation logic directly and locally in the in-network module, to reduce the control plane traffic under DoS. In addition, it is easy to implement, does not require to change the switch architecture, and can be easily integrated into NFV platforms.

## 6.5 CONCLUSION

The Control Plane Saturation (CPS) is a DoS attack being capable to significantly disrupt the operation of SDN, a rapidly growing networking model. The adversary, taking the advantage of SDN design primitives, floods the data plane with flow packets not matching the stored flow rules. As a consequence, floods of control packets are exchanged between the switch and controller.

We presented INFAS, a defense scheme for protecting SDN against CPS and counter abusive usage of the control plane resource. INFAS is installed on the rapidly increasing in-network commodity servers which are used in modern networks mainly to support NFV. The switch forwards the flow packets that do not match any of its concrete flow rules to a nearby INFAS module. INFAS evaluates these packets, and accordingly decides either to return them to the corresponding switches or to drop them.

Through a representative prototype and extensive emulations, we showed that INFAS is highly effective against CPS. In particular, it can decrease the amount of malicious control packets by up to 80%. The results also show that INFAS can improve the switch throughput by about 26%, when compared to the approaches of directly handling control packets on the controller side.

The current design of INFAS can be improved in several ways. In particular, we will investigate approaches to adjust INFAS parameters in an adaptive way, for different types of SDN networks. Another idea for investigation is to support cooperation among multiple INFAS modules to improve detection and mitigation of Distributed Denial of Service (DDoS).

CHAPTER 7

## CONCLUSION

Computer networks serve as the fundamental infrastructure that supports many facets of modern digital societies. Network softwarization, which is enabled by software defined networking and network functionality virtualization, provides a flexible method to implement and manage computer networks in the era of big data. In particular, SDN centralizes the control logics of a network, and takes advantage of the global view of the network operation status and usage. The different network planes, including data, monitoring and control planes, have their own unique type of resources. These resources can be unwisely even abusively used by end hosts and applications, which leads to degraded performance and increases operation cost. The strategies to optimize the resource consumption of SDN should adapt to the ever changing volatile environment.

The use of the SDN technology enables not only dynamic planning of network flow paths but also joint optimization across network layers. In SDN, a controller continuously collects monitoring information of network operation and network usage, and uses centralized algorithms to compute policies that adaptively configure a network. The interaction between a network controller and controllable entities, such as networking devices and management software components, is achieved using control messages.

SDN provides flexible network management and traffic engineering for optimization of the resource utilization of a network. Due to the complexity of nowday's network architecture, it is very challenging for a single framework to address all resource efficiency issues in every layer or functional plane of a network. This book focuses on unique resource types of important network functional planes. Mores specifically, it addresses the bandwidth efficiency in the monitoring plane, the power efficiency in the data plane and abusive usage of the control plane resource.

Despite the existence of several solutions addressing the above mentioned resource efficiency issues, there exist still several major. First of all, although adapting the routing paths of data flows can fulfill a specific network resource optimization goal, it always has negative impacts. For example, instead of the shortest paths, using alternative paths for the purpose of traffic aggregation or path stretching increases the resource consumption in the data forwarding plane and experienced delays. These negative impacts are usually negalected by existing work. Secondly, as the architecture of SDN has been extended to consist of heterogeneous communication technologies, e.g., wireless links along with wired ones, the approaches proposed to conserve resources for the classical SDN cannot be directly applied due to newly emerging conditions and constraints. Thirdly, the demand for adaptive network management increases when facing highly dynamic network workload and diverse network optmization goals. Classical approaches based on the optimization theory have the drawback of large computation time, and the ones based on heuristic algorithms requires in-depth understanding of the properties, e.g., topology, of a network. Lastly, due to the centralized architecture of SDN, the controller that execute traffic scheduling and network management algorithms becomes the target of the saturation attacks.

In this book, we develop frameworks, models and algorithms to address above described challenges. Particularly, this book makes the following contributions:

- *Conserve bandwidth resource in the monitoring plane (Chapter 3).* We presented REMO, a resource-efficient monitoring framework that conserves the bandwidth resource in the monitoring plane, with consideration of the negative impact of the commonly used path stretching approach.

- *Conserve power resource in the data plane (Chapter 4).* We introduced ECAS, a joint energy-efficient scheduling framework for hybrid micro data center networks equipped with both wired and directional wireless connections.

- *Conserve resource with self-adaptive algorithms (Chapter 5).* We investigated the possibility of using the state-of-the-art deep reinforcement learning algorithms to improve the power efficiency in SDN-based data center networks.

- *Mitigate abusive usage of the resource in the control plane (Chapter 6).* We designed INFAS, an in-network flow management scheme to protect the SDN control plane against denial-of-service attacks that intend to exhaust its valuable resources, such as bandwidth and computation resource of a controller.

The rests of this chapter summarize the main contributions of this book, discuss their limitations, and sketch possible and interesting directions for future work. Finally, we conclude this book with remarks.

## 7.1 CONTRIBUTIONS

In our first contribution, we addressed the bandwidth resource conservation in the monitoring plane of a network. The commonly used traffic engineering based approaches to reduce resource consumption incurred by a SDN monitoring system, is to alter the original shortest paths of data flows. The purpose of using alternative flow paths is to create opportunities to perform operations, such as extraction of aggregated monitoring data of different flows, to reduce the resource consumption in the monitoring plane. However, the selected alternative paths are mostly longer than the shortest ones, which actually leads to the wast of the transmission resources in the data plane and end-to-end delays. We proposed the REMO framework to address this defect of the current traffic engineering based resource conservation mechanism for the monitoring plane in SDN. REMO optimizes the total bandwidth resource consumption in both monitoring and data planes. We built an optimization model and a near-optimal heuristic algorithm based on the deflection technique to determine places of packet monitors, locations of mirroring traffic flows and their alternate paths. The simulation results show that our model and algorithm are able to achieve smaller amount of the total bandwidth resource consumption compared with randomized or mixed strategies. In order to describe the relative importance of the bandwidth resource in the monitoring and data planes, we introduced a configurable parameter named the link cost ratio. The experiment also proves that our algorithms are able to effectively reduce the length of alternative paths of data flows when the bandwidth in the monitoring and data plane has the equal or similar importance.

The second contribution of this book addresses the power resource conservation in the data plane of a network. The widely considered setups of a network to reduce the power consumption are either backbone networks or data center networks that have the traditional topology like fat-tree. We considered a hybrid and server-centric software-defined computer cluster architecture. In this newly proposed architecture, servers take responsibility of computation and packet forwarding, and they are interconnected by both wired links and directional wireless links. The power efficiency is achieved by putting unnecessary nodes and links of a network into the sleeping mode. In order to compute power-efficient configurations, we proposed the ECAS framework that contains the optimization model and heuristic algorithms to jointly schedule: (i) the directions of transmitting/receiving antennas used by wireless links, (ii) operation status (on/off status) of nodes and links in the network, (iii) routing paths of incoming flows. The simulation results show that, compared with the classical routing algorithms for the 3D torus architecture, our proposed model and algorithm is able to achieve maximum 33% more power conservation. Comparing with an energy-efficient routing algorithm that only considers power efficiency, our proposed heuristic algorithm is able to achieve slightly worse performance in power reduction but generates shorter transmission paths for flow packets.

In the third contribution of this book, we investigated the approach of using one type of the self-adaptive algorithms, deep reinforcement learning, to reduce power consumption for SDN-based data center networking. The power-efficiency problem in SDN is traditionally formulated and solved by using the optimization model and heuristic algorithm. These algorithms have strict constraints, thus not every possible set of input data can be solved, which leads to the failure of computation. Deep reinforcement learning has wider acceptance of input data due to its capability of approximation. As a result, we designed a DRL-based framework, named DeepGreen, to perform optimization on the power efficiency of DCN with the standard fat-tree architecture. Instead of using link-weight-based formulation, DeepGreen selects from the precomputed shortest flow paths and relies on a DRL algorithm designed for multiple agents. The goal is to preserve the shortest paths and reduce accumulated processing delays along paths. The evaluation results show that the current model in DeepGreen cannot compete with classical algorithms in reducing power consumption, but it maintains relatively low packet delays. The performance of DeepGreen, however, can further improve by following the detailed discussion of the evaluation results, as well as the suggested research directions described in Section 7.2.

In the last contribution of this book, we focus on the abusive usage of the resources in the SDN control plane. In particular, we considered the Denial-of-Service attacks that explore the control mechanism defined in the widely used SDN protocol, OpenFlow. The large amount of newly arrived flow packets, that have well-crafted inter-arrival time, trigger the switches in a SDN network to generate corresponding control messages. Excessive volumes of such control messages exhaust valuable SDN control plane resource, such as the bandwidth of the control channel between a controller and switches, and the computation resource of them. Since most of the control plane protection mechanisms are implemented on the controller side, these malicious incoming packets still have to be firstly converted into control messages and then analyzed by the protection module in the controller, which leads to reaction time that at least equals to the round-trip time between the SDN controller and switches. In this contribution, we proposed to implement a DoS mitigation mechanism for the SDN control plane as one of the many network functions that operate at the close proximity of each switch. To this end, we proposed a simple yet effective DoS mitigation algorithm that analyzes the incoming data packets and determines a dropout rate for their senders depending on the severity of their attacking behaviors. The evaluation shows that our proposed mechanism is able to effectively reduce the excessive volumes of control messages converted from attacking flow packets, which mitigates the abusive usage of the control plane resource. Meanwhile, due to the fact that different percentages of attacking flow packets are filtered out even before they trigger the generation of control messages, the throughput of switches under protection is also improved.

## 7.2 LIMITATIONS AND FUTURE DIRECTIONS

In this section, we discuss of the work presented in this book and suggest possible directions for future research.

MODEL AND PREDICT NETWORK TRAFFIC PROPERTIES    Monitoring network traffic and deriving models from collected historical data are able to characterize the properties of traffic flows. The derived models usually embed certain patterns of network traffic in the dimensions of time and space. The network optimization models and algorithms proposed in this book are reactive approaches, which require information of incoming traffic demands. As discussed in Section 2.2.3, in an idea SDN-assisted traffic engineering approach, such information is provided by the network resource provisioner that explicitly communicates with a cloud controller of a multi-tenant cloud environment or a data transfer controller of a big data analytical application. But there are still many scenarios where information of traffic demands cannot be directly obtained. Meanwhile, as the standard of data privacy enhances for cloud or network operators, the information of the internal states of an application may not be shared with the network controller. Proposing accurate network traffic models by using not only traditional statistical approaches but also state-of-the-art neural network based methods may help overcoming the unavailability of explicit traffic information. Additionally, these models can also predict the evolution of network traffic so as to enable proactive resource scheduling and network management.

HANDLING TRANSIENT CHANGES IN TRAFFIC PATTERNS  Even though network traffic models are able to characterize and predict their behaviors, it is very challenging to achieve very high accuracy, especially for short-term traffic prediction. As the micro-service architecture becomes popular in modern networks especially in the cloud environment, the application types become diverse and their life cycles are dynamic. The transient changes in traffic, such as microbursts in data center networks [248], requires additional reactive mechanisms to fast adapt network configurations in addition to the periodic and batch-based scheduling approaches proposed in this book. For example, besides the scheduling algorithms operated at the level of data flows, a caching mechanism to smooth the data rates of a flow that has been already placed on certain links is able to further avoid congestions caused by such burst transmission of packets. Another possible approach is that a switch or packet forwarding node that detects such transient changes in traffic pattern should use an extension of SDN control messages to inform the network controller.

LEARNING THROUGH KNOWLEDGE TRANSFER  A complex network optimization task is difficult to solve by directly applying the methodology of reinforcement learning due to the enormously large exploration space, which is the most important factor that prohibits the further improvement of system performance in Chapter 5. Instead of learning from the scratch, transferring knowledge of network control strategies made by other existing management algorithms to the learning agent is an interesting direction for future research. Transfer learning techniques have been used successfully in supervised learning tasks and now attract many attentions in deep reinforcement learning. It has been shown that transfer learning in reinforcement learning is able to improve the system performance and shorten training time [128, 212]. Among possible transfer learning paradigms in reinforcement learning [62], combining supervised learning or semi-supervised learning with RL is the most interesting one. In this method, the historical decisions made by classical network management algorithms can be used for supervised or semi-supervised learning.

The RL agent can improve its adaptivity and accuracy by training upon the pre-training results.

PRIORITIZE CONTROL PLANE RESOURCE ACCESS    In the next generation of communication networks, achieving low latency is one of the key performance requirements. Although the countermeasure developed in this book is able to mitigate abusive usage of the control plane resource, it cannot distinguish data flows that require priority in the competition for the control plane resource. Without considering the priority in accessing control plane resource, the data flows with the low-latency requirement have to suffer from queueing delays for generating and transmitting control messages as well as for computation on the controller, even under an attacking-free scenario. As a result, it is a future work to extend our proposed in-network flow packet management framework so that it is able to provide the low-latency guarantee in the control plane for data flows under both attacking and attacking-free scenarios.

## 7.3    CONCLUDING REMARKS

Software-defined networking enables flexible cross-layer network management. The resource existing in different functional planes of SDN should be intelligently and securely utilized. This book contributes to the design of resource-efficient SDN by conserving and protecting resources of its different functional planes.

APPENDIX A

---

APPENDIX

---

## A.1 USING MULTI-AGENT DRL AS A GENERIC TE FRAMEWORK

Multi-agent DRL formulation presented in Chapter 5 is expected to serve as a generic optimization framework of traffic engineering. In addition to previous discussed network optimization goal, reducing power consumption, another important traffic engineering objective is to reduce end-to-end delays in the network. In Chapter 5, this objective is configured as the secondary goal in the reward function. By extending the reward function, the multi-agent DRL formulation can be used to optimize a network to achieve different traffic engineering goals.

In this part, we provide a simple extension of the multi-agent DRL formulation to enable the optimization of these two traffic engineering objectives: reducing end-to-end delays and conserving power network power consumption. In the rest of this section, we refer these two TE objectives as G1 and G2 correspondingly. The approaches of modelling obvserved states and actions in the formulation has been presented in Section 5.4.4. In order to achieve the TE objectives, G1 and G2, the reward function for each agent can be modified as:

$$r = \begin{cases} -\beta * d, \text{TE objective is G1} \\ P_{total} - P(a) - \alpha * d, \text{TE objective is G2} \end{cases} \tag{A.1}$$

If the TE objective is configured as reducing end-to-end delays (G1), we simply multiply a factor $\beta$ and the maximum delay d experienced by packets of each flow, and the negative value of this multiplication result represents the reward for G1. If the TE objective is configured as conserving power network power consumption (G2), the final reward is represented as a weighted sum of the total amount of conserved power consumption and the maximum delay experienced by packets of a flow, which is the same as described in Section 5.4.4. $P_{total}$ stands for the total power consumption if all devices and links in the network are configured in the active mode. The action a represents the selected routing path for a pair of end nodes in the network. $P(a)$ is the power consumption for activating devices and links that belong to any selected path in the action a. Thus, $P_{total} - P(a)$ represents the total amount of conserved power consumption. To avoid the happening of

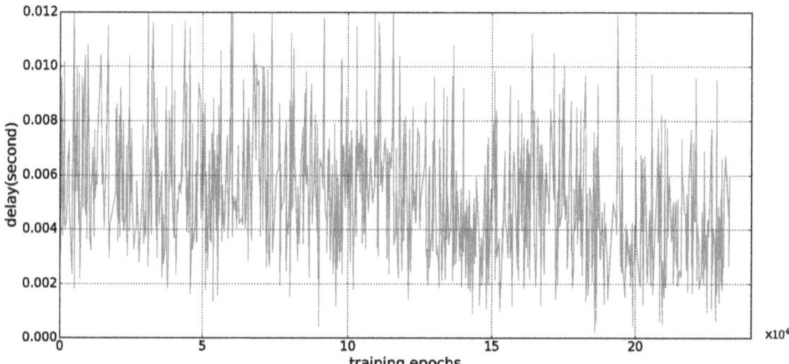

*(a)* The TE objective is configured as reducing end-to-end delays (G1). It shows the average maximum delays experienced by packets of all flows during training.

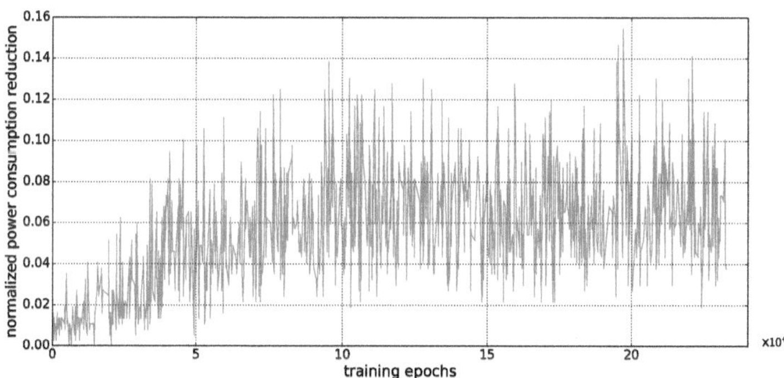

*(b)* he TE objective is configured as conserving power network power consumption (G2). It shows the normalized power consumption reduction during training.

*Figure A.1:* Performance of using multi-agent DRL formulation as a generic TE framework for two objectives.

assigning too much traffic workload to the same link, we subtract $\alpha * d$ from the the total amount of conserved power consumption, where $\alpha$ is a weight value.

We use the simulation framework developed in Chapter 5 to evaluate the performance of our multi-agent formulation in terms of achieving G1 and G2. The parameters used in the network simulation and neural networks are same as described in Section 5.5.1. In this evaluation, we configure the number of training epochs as $24 * 10^4$ to allow the maximum stability of training. It takes around 14 days on a regular desktop PC to complete one round of simulation. Two weight values, $\beta$ and $\alpha$, are configured as 100 and 300 respectively.

Figure A.1a shows the evaluation result when the TE objective is configured as G1. In particular, it depicts the average maximum delays experienced by packets of all flows during the training process. The average value of maximum experienced delays of all flows shows the descending trend. More specifically, it decreases from an average value of 0.0058 second in the first $13 * 10^4$ epochs to an average value of 0.0042 second after the $18 * 10^4$ epochs. This is around 27% reduction of the end-to-end delays.

Figure A.1b shows the evaluation result when the TE objective is configured as G2. In particular, it depicts the normalized power consumption reduction during the training process. This figure shows that the training process starts from the states where the flow paths are dispersed. It is the opposite of the state where the flows are consolidated and the power conservation is maximized. As the training continues, the percent of reduced power consumption increases until there is almost no further improvement. Our muti-agent DRL formulation achieves around 7% of power reduction. The training process becomes relatively stable after $10 * 10^4$ epochs.